Kiss Me in the

Coral Lounge

 DOUBLEDAY * NEW YORK

Kiss Me in the Coral Lounge

INTIMATE CONFESSIONS
FROM A HAPPY MARRIAGE

Helen Ellis

All rights reserved. Published in the United States by
Doubleday, a division of Penguin Random House LLC,
New York, and distributed in Canada by Penguin Random
House Canada Limited, Toronto.

www.doubleday.com

DOUBLEDAY and the portrayal of an anchor with a dolphin
are registered trademarks of Penguin Random House LLC.

Front-of-jacket illustration by Joanna Avillez / Illustration Division
Jacket design by John Fontana
Book design by Pei Loi Koay

LIBRARY OF CONGRESS CATALOGING-IN-PUBLICATION DATA
Names: Ellis, Helen, author.
Title: Kiss me in the Coral Lounge: intimate confessions
    from a happy marriage / Helen Ellis.
Description: First edition. | New York: Doubleday, [2023]
Identifiers: LCCN 2022036861 (print) | LCCN 2022036862
    (ebook) | ISBN 9780385548205 (hardcover) |
    ISBN 9780385548212 (ebook)
Subjects: LCSH: Ellis, Helen. | Marriage—New York
    (State)—New York. | Couples—New York (State)—New
    York.
Classification: LCC HQ557.N5 E45 2023 (print) | LCC HQ557.
    N5 (ebook) | DDC 306.8109747/1—dc23/eng/20220809
LC record available at https://lccn.loc.gov/2022036861
LC ebook record available at https://lccn.loc.gov/2022036862

MANUFACTURED IN THE UNITED STATES OF AMERICA

10 9 8 7 6 5 4 3 2 1

First Edition

For Victoria Buckley Curran,

who has heard every word

Hello, you have reached 212-734-_ _ _ _

Please leave a message for Lex or Helen

—RADIOSHACK ANSWERING MACHINE,

2001—2021

$\mathcal{C}$ontents

CONTENTS

Kiss Me in the

Coral Lounge

My Husband Snores

and Yours Will Too

A bear walked into a jewelry store and nobody was bothered but me. Well, it *was* Vegas. The bear was on a leash like a six-hundred-pound dog. The woman walking him had trained him like a dog. The bear sat by a display case of diamond earrings. The bear was motionless, but it growled. It *grow-uuuled*. And it *grow-uuuled*. Everybody kept shopping, but I was frozen. Because there was a bear in a jewelry store. It *grow-uuuled*. And it *grow-uuuled*.

And then I woke up.

My husband's snoring works its way into my dreams. I've dreamed I was watching a parade and his snoring was Shriners. I've dreamed I was on *The Price Is Right* and his snoring was the wheel. I've dreamed I was on safari and his snoring was lions eating a little girl. Yeah, the dreams ain't always good.

My husband didn't always snore. At least we don't think he did. I first became aware of it in our early forties, more than ten years into our marriage, after I went to a doctor to have wax cleaned out of my ear.

The doctor said, "Gotcha!"

I heard a *kerplunk* as a wad of wax, which had made me partially deaf—for I don't know how long—fell out of my ear and into a kidney-shaped dusty rose yurp tub like petrified Hubba Bubba chiseled out from under a desk.

And then I heard birds chirp over bus brakes outside the doctor's ground-floor office window. And then I heard his receptionist's gold bracelets jangle as she reached for my check. When I got home, I heard the oven preheat light click off once it reached 350 degrees. And *that* night, I heard my husband snore.

His snoring grew louder in the winter because our air conditioner—which buzzes like a microwave nuking a tinfoil swan full of leftovers—was turned off. His snoring grew more frequent when the apartment was dry. His snoring is now nearly nightly, my husband claims, because he's put on weight (he looks the same to me). But I think the culprit is age.

All my middle-aged friends' middle-aged husbands sound like they're chainsawing crackers in bed. How do I know? Because this is what we talk about when we talk about our husbands. Snoring and skin tags and prostates and knees.

Just this week my friend Erica introduced me to her friend Cynthia at lunch and Cynthia said, "My husband doesn't snore, he *pooh-poohs*. As he's going to sleep, he makes this little *pfft* or *poof* sound."

"So does mine," I said.

"Oh my god, so does mine!" Erica said.

Cynthia said, "I pinch his lips together with my fingers, but he *pffts* or he *poofs* out the side of his mouth."

No, nasal strips don't work. If you can convince your husband to wear one—which, depending on your husband, can be akin to him convincing you to go night-night in a wrought iron chastity belt—the strip peels off, or worse, turns him into a mouth breather. More than once, I have dreamed I was being seduced by Darth Vader.

So we kick them and feign sleep. Oh yes, we've all done it. They stop snoring because we've kicked them. Or pinched their nostrils or pushed their bodies off the bed. I know women who've punched their husbands in the back. My personal preference is to hoist my lower half into mid-air and slam it down on the mattress. Or gyrate in place. Our husbands wake up, and we pretend that they have woken *themselves* up. Because we are sleeping soundly. *See how our eyes are closed and we are breathing slowly? See how we don't respond to accusations or pokes?* I have never faked an orgasm, but I can play dead. I've watched enough survivalist and true crime shows to know how to roll into a ball so a moose bats you around but then leaves you alone, or go limp so a serial killer who's killed all your sorority sisters walks out of Phi Mu because he thinks he's killed you, too.

But none of this is a long-term solution, so we do our best to live with it.

We buy earplugs. And let me tell you: there are many different kinds of earplugs on the market. I ended up favoring the "pink ones," which you are instructed to twist before slipping into your ears. As soon as they're in there, you feel them expanding like spray foam that exterminators use to clog mouse holes. It sounds creepy and it feels creepy, but what are you going to do? Keep those earplugs in your bedside drawer like antacid or Viagra, that's what you're going to do. Because bedside drawers are full of hope. And I'm sorry to dash yours: earplugs muffle but don't mute the noise. They fall out of your ears and find their way into your armpits.

We build pillow forts. We put pillows over our heads. We pull covers over our heads. We tamp our bodies down with weighted blankets that some folks use to weather thunderstorms. We drink. We take drugs. We wear headphones and listen to podcasts; many of us fall asleep to other women discussing *other* women's murders because we would rather hear recaps about dismemberment, cannibalism, and skin suits than snoring.

We buy sound machines. And let me tell you: there are many different kinds of sound machines on the market.

Some sound like frogs, some sound like forests, sometimes an owl hoots, but I don't find any of this relaxing. Same goes for oceans and dolphins: they make me want to pee. I chose the sound machine that my shrink has by her door so that no one in the waiting room can hear you crying. Or it's there to make *you think* nobody in the waiting room can hear you crying because you can't hear them. I'm sorry to inform you: we can hear you in the waiting room. If I had a few hundred bucks for every time I politely didn't look up from my book when a patient came red-faced out of my shrink's office, I could afford therapy without health insurance.

My sound machine looks like a deflated volleyball and *whirrrrs.* If you flick the switch to the second level, it *whirrrrs* a little louder. Every night, I curl toward it like a puppy in a cardboard box curls toward a ticking clock meant to simulate its mother's heartbeat.

The problem is, sound machines *compete* for your attention. Like when you cover your ears—because someone is telling you something you don't want to know about—and you go, "La la la, I can't hear you!"

Some of my friends lean into the theory of more noise and create a cacophony of kids, cats, and dogs by hollering, "Everybody in the bed!"

My friend Mary Jo says, "My three fur babies [aka a golden retriever, a black lab, and a German shepherd] actually sleep in their own beds on the floor in our bedroom, but they snore just as loud as my husband does, so it sounds like a motorcycle rally."

Some of our husbands have gone so far as to go under the knife.

My friend Heather's husband had surgery on his palate. She says, "He had something wrong, something hung down wrong or something like that. I can't recall the details, but it worked for a few years and then the snoring came back, which was expected, the doctor said, if he gained weight as he aged."

Another friend's husband had "a nose job without a nose job" to fix his deviated septum, but his snoring came back too. To add insult to injury, he says, "I don't do well with anesthesia, I always wake up. I woke up in my colonoscopy and fought the nurses. This time I woke up to the *crunch* when they broke my nose."

My friend Jean struggled with her husband's snoring for eight years until she laid down an ultimatum. She said, "If you don't get a sleep study, I'm going to stab you with a knife or divorce you. I'll tell the judge I'm a crackhead and leave you with the kids."

A sleep study is spending the night in a hotel room, except that there are doctors watching you through cameras and monitoring your vitals. A sleep study is to find apnea. Apnea means you stop breathing while you snore, which means you get as close to death without really dying until the one day you *do* die, right next to your partner. The anxiety of you dying with your head on the neighboring pillow keeps your partner awake at night because when she hears you stop snoring, she holds *her* breath until you bolt upright back to life like a zombie who heard a twig snap.

My friend Erica's husband's sleep study was cut short after only three hours because he'd already stopped breathing more than thirty times each hour. The doctors gave him a CPAP machine, which he has used ever since.

A continuous positive airway pressure machine is a nose mask attached to headgear with "elbows" that looks like the Facehugger that sat on that astronaut's face in *Alien*. There is a hose that runs off it like a tail and connects to a machine that looks like a cassette clock radio. The good news is, your husband doesn't snore. The bad news is, he looks like an invalid.

Erica's husband straps his on when he gets into bed with a book so he can fall asleep reading.

Jean's husband has one for home and one for travel.

Heather says her husband's CPAP saved their marriage.

But the machine doesn't work for everyone. Some husbands get claustrophobia. Some husbands get chapped cheeks or nosebleeds. For some, it's a vanity issue. And if you don't clean the hose, it gurgles.

My friend whose husband got the non–nose job says, "Now, when his snoring wakes me up, I gingerly get out of bed and go sleep in the guest room."

Another friend says she and her husband get in the same bed each night, but as they get sleepy he "retires" to another room.

Grandmother and Granddaddy slept in separate rooms directly across the hall from each other. Hers was powder blue: powder-blue carpet, powder-blue curtains, powder-blue bedspread, powder-blue paint. She slept on a powder-blue satin "style saver" pillow with a neck gulley to prevent her weekly perm-and-set from getting mussed. By her bedside was a hardback like *The Shell Seekers* or *The Other Side of Midnight* and beside that was a 1970s brass princess phone as heavy as an anvil. Granddaddy's bedroom was dark green and smelled like Old Spice. Next to his bed was a pack of cigarettes and a police scanner. I don't know why they slept separately—maybe he snored— but as far as I know, they were happily married.

Mama had a sleep study when she was in her sixties. She didn't have apnea, she had night terrors. She was recorded howling and flailing her legs ninety-eight times in an hour. She was given medication to stop her nightmares, but I can attest that those pills don't work. When my sister, Elizabeth, and I returned home to Alabama for Papa's open-heart surgery, he recovered upstairs in one bedroom, while Elizabeth slept on an air mattress in front of the big TV outside his door. I slept with Mama in a bedroom downstairs.

In the morning I asked my sister, "Did you hear Mama screaming all night long?"

"No, Helen Michelle. All I heard was *you* screaming, HUSH, MAMA! HUSH, MAMA!"

My friend Laurie, who's never "slept right," bought a phone app to see if she had apnea. The app records noises while you sleep. The app didn't record Laurie snoring, it recorded her laughing.

"Maniacally," said Laurie. "All night long like the Wicked Witch of the West."

"Your husband never told you?" I asked.

"No," said Laurie. "*He* sleeps like a log. And bless his heart, he doesn't snore."

For my fortieth birthday, my family got together in New Orleans to celebrate. We stayed at the Hotel Monteleone, and my parents got separate rooms. Papa and I had lunch a block away at the Acme Oyster House bar, where unprompted by me he said, "You know, Helen Michelle, just because your mother and I sleep in separate rooms doesn't mean I don't love her very much."

"Okay," I said. "Please pass the Crystal hot sauce."

When my husband and I got COVID-19 in December 2020, we slept in separate rooms for two weeks. He had *the cough* and I had *the fever*. He slept on the sofa in the TV room—which we call "the Coral Lounge" because we painted it a deliriously warm shade of pinkish orange—

and I slept in our bed with our two cats, who snuggled up to me like I was a hot water bottle.

When we got back in bed together, my husband and I confessed that we'd slept better apart than we had slept together in years. I didn't wake up because I didn't hear him snoring. He didn't wake up because I didn't wake him up to stop him from snoring.

"Wanna do it?" I whispered.

"I could do it," he said.

Drifting off to sleep, pillow-talking in the moonlight, we fantasized about a future that included two bedrooms as if it was the most illicit idea that we'd ever had.

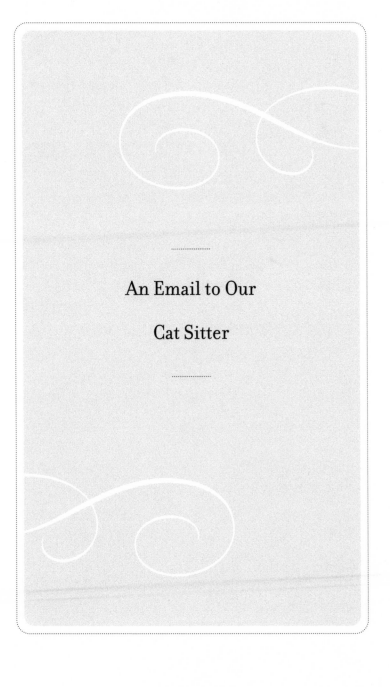

An Email to Our

Cat Sitter

Hello and welcome to New York!

THANK YOU for apartment sitting and taking care of our cats. All you REALLY have to do is keep them alive and NEVER open the windows from the bottom because the cats might jump out. The rest of this is finer points. Enjoy yourself!

Once you are inside our apartment, go to the kitchen and open the cabinet to the left of the fridge. There are cat bowls and cans of cat food in the top drawer. There are also "wet pouches," which are "meat and gravy" in Capri Sun–looking bags that you rip open and squeeze like you're wringing out your bathing suit. Give each boy a can or a wet pouch in a fresh dish. If they eat out of a dirty dish, the orange one will get "chin acne" and the old one will barf.

If you hear the old one barfing, please "direct" him off the rugs and onto the hardwood or tiled floors, where the barf will be easier to clean up. He only barfs like once a week. And sometimes he barfs because he's been waiting for you to feed him and then eats too quickly. So don't make him wait. Honestly, when this old cat "asks" for food, give it to him. I don't care if you fed him five minutes ago and he ate one bite. If he only ate one bite, he wants the canned or pouch food that you didn't give him. So switch it out. We are not concerned about training or putting a sixteen-year-old cat on a diet. We are only concerned with keeping him happy. If he is not happy, he will let you know by pooping in the tub.

"Asking" for food includes meowing at the top of his lungs from the kitchen counter or staring at you from the coffee table like he's trying to suck your soul out. Sometimes we feed him ON the coffee table because he "likes to be part of things" and sometimes he won't eat unless you "keep him company" by sitting on the kitchen floor and petting him and singing him an eating song. I've made up a song, but you can sing ANYTHING. My husband just says "Good boy" repeatedly and the cat eats fine.

When you eat, the old cat will want to eat what you're eating, so use the squirt bottle to squirt him away until you've finished your meal. The squirt bottle was originally bought to spritz the plants, but now we spritz the plants in the shower because JUST THE SOUND of the squirt bottle will set the old cat off like a firecracker. He may also go berserk at the sound of a sneeze. So far it's just my husband's sneezes that he "reacts" to. If I sneeze, he doesn't flinch, but if my husband sneezes, the old cat charges him, climbs him, and swats him across the face. My husband assures me it doesn't hurt, it's just startling. So when you feel a sneeze coming on, go on the defensive and step into a closet.

When you finish a meal, please put your leftovers on the coffee table. Even if there's just a speck of sauce left on your dish, please give it to the old cat because he likes to lick the "essence." The only thing he can't eat is spaghetti (choking hazard) and spicy (DON'T ASK).

The orange cat couldn't care less what you're eating. He "keeps to himself" until about nine at night when he's ready for his dry food. The orange cat is a genius and extremely well-mannered. If you see him sitting quietly by an empty bowl in the TV room (aka the Coral Lounge), this means he's ready for his "late-night snack." There is a seven-pound bag of dry food labeled "Indoor Adult" RIGHT OUT IN THE OPEN in the Coral Lounge. Some people have asked if it's modern art like one of those Andy Warhol Brillo boxes, but it really is just a humongous bag of cat food that we leave out because, as my husband says, "It's just easier that way."

The same sentiment applies to the fourteen-pound bag of cat litter labeled "Clumping Unscented" that we leave right out in the open next to the litter box in our bathroom like some people don't think twice about leaving out their plunger.

You will know when the old cat has pooped, because he POOPS AND RUNS! If he's running from room to room like a cartoon bullet bouncing off the walls, and you didn't spritz the squirt bottle or sneeze, that means he just pooped. There are special green bags to scoop the poop, but if he didn't bury it feel free to pick it up with toilet paper and flush it down the toilet. Please praise the old cat when he doesn't have diarrhea. I've made up another song for this, but you can say ANYTHING. My husband just says "Nice job" repeatedly and the old cat is "very proud of himself."

If you want to air out the bathroom, please remember to crack the window from the top not the bottom, but there also is a three-wick "salted grapefruit" candle that is guaranteed to kill the odor. If the old cat pees in the tub, I run hot water to wash it down the drain and at the same time douse it with a thirty-ounce gift bottle of Jean Naté (there is a reason Revlon still makes this product: it is a miracle worker). But you can use ANYTHING. The orange cat is so considerate, I swear he poops potpourri.

I know that some people are of the mind that "if it's yellow, let it mellow" and don't flush their toilets to conserve water, but this is not such a household. The cats drink out of the toilets. So please flush them every time you use them and leave the lids up. If you sit on a wet seat, the seat is wet from the cats' paws because they submerge their front paws in the basin to drink, and then take their wet paws out to TRAIPSE around the seat and go back in again. If you happen upon one of their deep dives (a cat butt sticking out of the toilet), back away slowly. You don't want to startle them. Trust me, you don't.

The cats do have a proper water bowl, so even though this sounds ridiculous, please change the water in it twice a day. You will NEVER see them drink out of it, but they MUST be doing it because the water level goes down. I mean, if they're not drinking out of it, WHAT is? It's not mice or rats, I promise. We haven't seen one of those in this apartment for years. We got the cats to get rid of the mice and "the lone rat." The orange one did all the work. The old one "helped" by glowering at the dark space under the oven for hours.

The cats will probably be hiding when you arrive, so when you enter the bedroom don't be alarmed by the two lumps under the comforter. Go ahead and say hello. Let them hear your voice. Pat the lumps. Lift up the comforter and let them see your face. They might dart out and go under the bed, but whatever the case, don't worry, they NEVER SCRATCH OR BITE. Just leave them be and settle in.

Hang your coat in the coat closet or the old cat will sit on it. Unpack and put your suitcases away or both cats will "nest" in them.

The cats are allowed to sit anywhere, but each have their "territories." Neutral territories are the bed and the two story "scratch tower" in the Coral Lounge. Otherwise, the old cat likes to "teeter" on the edges of sofas or "cook" by lying before the radiator with his paws slipped underneath, but he can mostly be found "holding court" in "his box," which originally contained a pair of mail-order khakis. When my husband opened this box on the dining room table, the old cat laid claim to it with such conviction that my husband did not return the pants, which were too big for him, and we have forever after eaten off our laps in the Coral Lounge.

The orange cat only sits on the royal blue velvet swivel chairs like the prince that he is. If you don't see him sitting there, you will know that he has been there by the mist of orange fur. To clean the fur, there is a teeth-tartar-yellow rubber "brick" that we drag across the velvet like a tongue scraper, but you can clean it with ANYTHING. We have lint rollers and an upright vacuum with five attachments.

Like I mentioned, the orange one "keeps to himself."

So if he "disappears," as long as you haven't opened the windows from the bottom, don't freak out. I promise he hasn't gone off to find a corner to die. There's no way he'll die before the old one.

If the cats fight, it will take less than a minute for them to "work it out," so don't get involved. If the cats are on the bed at bedtime and you don't "wrangle" them into the Coral Lounge, they will sleep with you. If you don't mind the old one "waking you up" by chewing your hair like a wistful farmer chews a hay straw at three a.m. because he wants another wet pouch, please by all means enjoy what my husband calls "family time."

The cats are very loving and I am sure you will enjoy them as much as we do. The old one likes to be kissed on the head. The orange one likes a little "roughhousing." The old one likes to be held like a baby: over your shoulder or rocked in your arms. The orange one likes to be carried face forward like a ventriloquist's doll. If you give the orange one "extra attention," the old one will "sense" it from the room he is in, skulk into the room that you and the orange one are in, and stare at you as if he is asking for food. What he is asking for is for you to stop what you are doing with the orange one and give him attention. Please do so. The orange one is okay with this.

As with any hundred-year-old building, this apartment has its "quirks." Meaning: there are many things that will make you think our apartment is haunted, but it is not haunted. The floors creak and the radiators clang because that's what floors and radiators do. There are "hot spots" on the walls because pipes are behind them. We have a lot of portrait paintings, but the eyes are not following you. If the lights go out, you've blown a fuse (you can only have three things turned on in a room at one time). The fuse box is in the stairwell.

If you meet a woman in the stairwell, do not engage with her. Don't even make eye contact. This woman LOOKS LIKE A GHOST, but she is not a ghost. She is one of three neighbor ladies. Neighbor Lady #1 is a widow and an opera singer who practices two hours every day whenever the mood strikes her, so when you hear waves of ear-piercing screeching, rest assured it's just this lady "doing her scales." Neighbor Lady #2 is a spinster and plays the piano every day whenever the mood strikes her, so when you hear what sounds like the single-note soundtrack to *Eyes Wide Shut,* it's just this lady "staying mentally sharp." Neighbor Lady #3 is (we're guessing) on her way to divorce and "likes her candles," which she burns nonstop when she is in town. Her scent of choice is not "salted grapefruit," so please don't fear that a hellmouth has opened up when you smell what (we're guessing) Yankee Candle Company would name "Satan's hooves."

Please help yourself to what's in the kitchen. The guest

towels are on the rack. Don't forget about not opening the windows from the bottom so the cats won't jump out. Text me with ANY questions. THANK YOU, THANK YOU!

We'll be back in two days,
Helen

What's in the Box?

On a Sunday morning in New York City, my husband stopped short on the sidewalk and said, "Oh my god, I can't believe I didn't tell you what happened last night on my walk with Rich."

My husband takes nightly walks with our friend Rich, who manages a bunch of buildings in Manhattan, so he is always getting a call about something that's gone wrong. Somebody's electricity is out, there's a small fire, there's a ceiling leak, there's a smell coming from an apartment and that smell ain't brisket. So more often than not on their walks, Rich stops at an apartment to fix what needs fixing.

Usually, when my husband gets home, I ask him, "Anything to report?"

"No, nothing."

"Nothing?"

"No, nothing. I'm sorry."

My husband hates to disappoint me. The man knows I love gossip.

But this time he had something. He said, "You're gonna be so happy when I tell you this, Helen. You're gonna love me so much!"

"Oh!" I clutched my hands to my chest. You know how cheerleaders go, *Ready? Okay!*

My husband said, "Rich and I stopped by this building that some people bought before the pandemic and never moved into, so it's been abandoned. We go in and when I say the place was dark, I mean it was *completely* dark. And it's dark outside and there's no power inside and I'm waiting for my eyes to adjust and I feel cobwebs and there's no furniture, but I'm making out shapes. I'm thinking, *There could be people squatting in here.*"

"Or ghosts," I said.

"I thought of that," he said. "The whole thing was straight out of a horror movie. Especially when Rich says, *I gotta go to the basement, do you wanna come with me?*"

I gasped the kind of gasp that leaves your face looking like a cornhole board.

"And I am telling you, Helen, you are gonna be so proud of me: I heard your voice in my head when I said, *No thank you.*"

"Good job!" I said. "Did you wait on the stoop?"

"No, I backed into a corner so nothing could sneak up

on me. I kept waiting for some figure to step out from behind a door. And then five minutes pass with Rich in the basement. And then ten minutes pass with Rich in the basement. And then I work up the nerve to walk over to the basement door and yell down, *Rich, are you okay?*

"*Yep!* he says. *Be right up!*

"And he comes out of the basement holding a shoe box. And I ask him, *What's in the box?*

"And Rich shrugs and says, *Guess.*

"So I guess: *Feces.*

"And Rich shakes his head no. Then he shakes the box and says, *Guess again.*

"But we are still in this house and all I want to do is get out of there, so I say, *Just tell me.*

"And Rich says, *Eh, I'll show you outside.*

"And when I saw it, I couldn't believe it. Helen, what's in the box?"

"Satanic talisman," I said.

"Nope."

"Fetus."

"Nope. I feel like I'm your father playing Five Dollar Mystery Box at one of his garage sales. Guess again, you'll never guess it."

I did not guess it.

When I *did* find out what was in the box, I marched my husband straight back to our apartment and made him call Mama in Alabama and tell her the story because Mama's side of the family are born storytellers and we appreciate when someone who's married into our group gives it a go.

The last time my husband was at a family gathering, my uncle Will, Mama's eighty-five-year-old brother and a retired history professor, told us about a high school classmate who'd murdered his grandmother with a refrigerator. And yes, Uncle Will told this twenty-minute story in front of three generations over a very public brunch. My husband had listened stoically while the rest of us had laughed and *laughed,* scarfing down our eggs Benedict.

Papa likes to say, "Your mother is such a good audience, she listens to a waiter list the specials like she's in the front row of a Rolling Stones concert."

The last time I made my husband call and tell Mama a story was in September 2020, after he'd been in Central Park on a Sunday morning and had stopped to listen to a guy play saxophone under a tree. There was a nip in the air, the leaves were changing colors, and an old man in a suit strolled toward them with a big handsome dog, maybe a Rottweiler, and my husband thought, *Oh what a nice New York City moment. There's a light at the end of the COVID-19 tunnel. New York City is still what it used to be.* Especially when the saxophonist shouted, "GET YOUR MOTHER-FUCKING DOG AWAY FROM ME!"

Mama had laughed and *laughed.* She loves it when my husband does voices.

When Mama heard the What's in the Box? story, she guessed, "Severed hand!"

My husband said, "Nope."

"Severed foot! Severed *foot!*"

"Nope."

Mama did not guess it.

When Mama *did* find out what was in the box, she laughed and *laughed.* My husband treats my mother with the utmost respect, so she loves it when he *crosses a line,* which is mother-in-law-speak for *broaches a subject as inappropriate as a googly-eyed titty lapel pin.*

My husband and I told every friend we came in contact with the What's in the Box? story because at long last we had a story to tell. It was June 2021, and for sixteen months, my husband and I had been "doing our part" by working from home and socializing outside in small groups at a distance. Every so often, six to eight of us would gather on Rich's roof, sit in a circle six to eight feet apart, and eat from paper bags of Sticky's fried chicken.

Our friends always had stories to tell. Michelle had had a baby one month before lockdown. Another friend ran the city's largest coronavirus testing site, which turned into the city's largest vaccination site. Another friend and her family had relocated to the Hamptons, where they were sure they'd bought the last house on the market: a lavish 1980s coke den that came with a basement full of a dead man's Christmas ornaments and a life-size stuffed horse that was also a lamp.

None of them guessed what was in the box.

We must have told thirty people the story because the story became a kind of psychological test. You know: What does your friend's guess say about your friend? And how does your friend's guess make you feel about *your* guess? Like when you look at an inkblot and see a vagina and are relieved to find out that all your friends see vaginas. Or you take that fill-in-the-blank test and finish incomplete sentences like "I regret (blank)." Or in our case, "I regret leaving my (blank) in a basement." I don't know what Schrödinger's cat experiment was supposed to prove with the question, Is the cat in the box alive or dead? but what it proved about our friends was that they are animal lovers. Nobody guessed there was a cat in there.

Our friends guessed: a wig, a dead baby's rattle, baby teeth, used Q-tips, fingernail clippings, ashes, dirty underwear, vintage porn, a snuff tape, lost love letters, and a still-beating heart.

Apparently we all expect the worst.

But my friend Donna guessed shoes were in the shoe box.

I said, "That's so logical!"

And my friend Erica guessed gold coins.

I said, "That's so optimistic!"

Erica said, "Actually, it's the opposite."

When she told the story to her sister, her sister guessed the same thing: gold coins.

Erica said, "I wonder if that's the standard answer of a Holocaust survivor's child? They sewed gold coins or diamonds into their clothing because they weren't allowed to bring their belongings. Refugees always need to be ready to run. Our family hid gold coins in the legs of the furniture. The furniture survived the war, was rescued from being stolen, and then shipped to my father's family in Israel."

Erica's answer showed my husband and me that we were ignorant. Perhaps willfully so.

My friend Dani loves games so much she nearly choked to death in a marshmallow mouth-stuffing contest. Oh yes, before our friend Jeremy gave her the Heimlich she told me she remembered thinking, *I'm dying. This is how I'm going to die: death by Chubby Bunny. And I'm kind of fine with it. At least I'll die doing something I love.* When the marshmallow flew out of her mouth, the first thing she said was, "I won."

Dani had the sense to ask me, "Was the item *in* the box to begin with, or did Rich find it and put it in the box to transport it?"

I said, "It was *outside* the box and he put it in the box to transport it. Does it matter?"

"Uh, yeah!"

All this time, we'd been telling it wrong.

Still, Dani did not guess it.

A week or so later, I ran into Rich and his wife, Susan, on the street. I said to Susan, "Can you believe what they found in the basement?"

Susan did not know what I was talking about.

I said to Rich, "You didn't tell her the What's in the Box? story?"

Rich did not know what I was talking about.

I started to tell them the story—the abandoned building, the basement, the box—and even though Rich is the main character, the hero of this hero's journey, there was no recognition on his face about what I was saying.

Susan was rapt.

I was flabbergasted.

I listed friends' answers.

Susan guessed: "Mice."

"Nope."

"A rat?"

Nope.

And *still* Rich had no idea what I was talking about.

And I thought, *Did my husband make up an elaborate lie to keep something even more sinister from me?*

And I said to Rich, "How is this not ringing any bells?"

"Oh right," Rich nodded. "Gigantic dildo."

Susan squealed.

I screamed, "Rich, how did you not remember that?"

Rich said, "Well, I *have* found dead bodies."

The first thing friends wanted to know *after* they found

out that there was a gigantic dildo in the box was, *Was it Rich's?* As if he'd been running some kind of underground sex ring and left it behind like a toothbrush at a Motel 6. The second question friends asked was, *What did Rich do with it?* Answer: He threw it in a city trash can.

My husband and I stopped telling the What's in the Box? story the day I helped my friend Martin hang art in his apartment. Holding up his mother's oil painting of a slice of chocolate cream pie, I told him about the abandoned building, the basement, the box—but this time made sure to mention that Rich spotted the item lying on the cold concrete floor and put it in the box to transport it because he didn't want to carry it in his bare hands.

Without missing a beat, Martin said, "Was it a dildo?"

Ding, ding, ding! Judge's ruling? Acceptable.

I qualified, "The correct answer is: a *gigantic* dildo."

Martin said, "Is there any other kind?"

I couldn't wait until I got home to tell my husband that someone had finally guessed right, so I texted him: "Dildo!"

My husband texted: "No way?! First guess?"

The best games always end with a winner. Martin officially won What's in the Box? So now it's over. Or is it? I'm the one who married a man who knew how happy this story would make me, who knew I'd appreciate it more than anyone and share it with everyone. I'm the one who got lucky. So I think the winner is me.

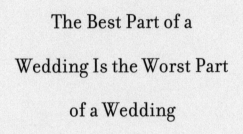

The Best Part of a

Wedding Is the Worst Part

of a Wedding

*T*wo days before my sister's wedding, Mama tripped in a Cracker Barrel parking lot and knocked out her front teeth.

"Your father *had* to have a piece of pie," Mama said.

They'd been driving from Birmingham to Asheville, North Carolina, where my sister, Elizabeth, and her fiancé, Stefan, were getting married. Fortunately, the Cracker Barrel where Mama landed on her face was near Athens, Georgia, where her brother, my uncle Will, knew a dentist, who saw her right away and did what he could to lodge her teeth back in place.

Mama arrived at our bed and breakfast high on pain-killers and wearing a surgical mask. Propped up in a four-poster bed, surrounded by dolls, doilies, Bradford Exchange collector plates, and our immediate family,

Mama granted my husband's request to drop her mask so he could see.

Mama looked like she'd taken up breakdancing without a carboard box. Her chin, cheeks, and nose were gravel burned; her porcelain skin bruised black and blue; her lips cut and swollen; her eyes crossed from the meds.

She asked my husband, "How bad is it?"

My husband can't lie worth a damn. The man is less animated than a documentary on soap. When he forced himself to smile, he looked like a jack-o'-lantern lit up by a black light: unnatural and bizarre.

He said through clenched teeth, "Ohhhh, it's okay, you look gooood."

Mama later said that this moment was when she realized how truly awful she looked.

My sister googled "Asheville drag queens" right there on the spot. She told Mama, "If they can cover a five o'clock shadow, they can cover what you got."

This is the first thing I think of when I think of my sister's wedding. Then I think of Mama wearing pearls and a Percocet to the rehearsal dinner, mingling with a man whom she thought was one of Stefan's Swedish relatives, slowing her southern accent to sound like the Beatles' "Revolution 9" played in reverse, until the man she was talking to ever-so-gently interrupted her to say, "Helen, I'm your cousin from Yazoo City."

And then I remember that minutes before my husband was to escort Mama down the aisle to her seat at the start of the wedding ceremony, he ripped the back of his Thom Browne suit from knee to crotch on a chair nail.

"Who has duct tape?" a groomsman yelled.

And please note that the question wasn't, "*Does* anyone have duct tape?"

Elizabeth and Stefan's friends were New York City sketch comedy people who went by the group names Meat and Elephant Larry. Several of them had duct tape on their person the way I always have at least three pencils in my purse.

"It was a waitress who helped me," my husband says when I tell him what I'm writing about.

"No it wasn't," I say. "It was one of the Jeffs. Jeff or Geoff, one of the guys who did the sketch about a blind date who was really a thousand mice in a person costume."

"Well, whoever it was," my husband says, "I appreciated it."

My husband maintained his composure as *somebody* sat between his spread legs and applied a strip of tape as long as a lawnmower cord.

When Mama took his arm, she said, "I know you did this on purpose to make me laugh."

My husband patted her hand and didn't say otherwise.

"See," Papa says, "when stuff like this happens, some

people see it as bad, but I think it's the stuff worth talking about. It's what makes a good love story. When I married your mother in her hometown, I remember the bride's side was packed, but only three people sat on my side—my parents and my grandmother—so some of the towns-people moved over to fill up my side and make my family feel better."

"Oh, that's so nice," I say. "Do you remember anything else about your wedding?"

"Yeah," Papa says. "When the priest asked your mother, 'Helen, do you take Mike?' her father objected."

Papa's real name is John. His *nickname* is Mike because when he was born his parents couldn't agree on a name. At some point, Granddaddy ducked out of the hospital for a sandwich and Grandmother called a nurse for the birth certificate and named him John Edward Jr. But Grand-daddy said, "One man going through life with this name is enough. I'm calling the kid Mike!"

Grandpapa, my mother's father, alleged that their mar-riage wouldn't be legal because the priest used Papa's nickname, Mike. But his objection was swiftly overruled by Papa's mother and grandmother, who had been respect-fully addressed all their married lives by their nicknames Boots and Honey.

I was late for my own wedding at the Greek cathedral on the Upper East Side of Manhattan because I couldn't get a taxi from the Midtown hotel where I'd spent the night.

Papa had walked over from his hotel to escort me and, standing on a street corner, I was frantic.

I waved a bouquet of red roses at unlit yellow cabs.

Papa said, "Helen Michelle, they're not going to start the wedding without you."

But I'd felt tested. Two nights before, the Greek restaurant where we'd booked our reception had burnt to the ground.

"It was a kitchen fire," my husband says.

"No it wasn't," I say. "It was arson. The whole place went up in smoke."

"Well, whatever it was," my husband says, "we weren't going to eat there."

Armed with the power of my secretarial Rolodex, I'd been able to secure a steak frites supper for fifty-four in the bordello-red basement of Rue 57.

Everybody has stories like these. Well, maybe not exactly like these. But ask yourself, ask *anybody*, "How was the wedding?" and the first thing worth talking about will be what went wrong. Because otherwise weddings are boring. No matter what the bridesmaids are forced to wear, or what music is played, or where the wedding takes place, or who performs the ceremony, or what kind of vows they do, or how they walk or electric slide or limbo up the aisle, or what kind of food is served, or what kind of bar it is, or how many tiers of cake there are, or how gently that cake is shoved into the bride's face, we have all been there and seen that. What we haven't seen is groomsmen mount the tables and dare one another to swallow goldfish from the goldfish bowl centerpieces. But we'd like to.

The best part of a wedding is the worst part of a wedding.

Remember? A veil caught fire, a groom fainted, a member of the wedding party fainted, somebody barfed, somebody boycotted at the last minute and catering didn't clear their empty chair, a wineglass was clinked and started a drunk-uncle-athon.

When handed a mic to make a toast, some people think it's their chance to be funny. Turns out they're closeted stand-ups and pull forty-five minutes of untested material out of their suit jacket pocket. I once heard a best man deliver a Best Man Checklist. He said, "Rings, vows, breath mints: check." And then the checklist took a cringeworthy turn. He said, "I was going to check the groom's zipper, but I know *his mom* always does that."

Hey, the happy couple can't control everything.

One friend got stuck in traffic for two hours on the Long Island Expressway on the way to her reception, and we bridesmaids piled out of a limousine onto the side of the road to hold up her princess skirt while she peed. Another friend fell off her chair during the hora. At another friend's wedding, all the men disappeared into a country club TV room to watch the Bama game, while her stepmother, clad in a gold lamé gown, danced alone in front of the band, stripping off her control-tops. In another friend's wedding video, his stepmother appears without panties, as he says, "doing the splits standing up," or as my friend in Florida would say, "showing everyone her *fine china.*"

This same friend in Florida says, "The mother of the groom's job is to shut up, show up, pay up, and wear beige."

Superstitious brides are supposed to carry something old, something new, something borrowed, something blue, and wear white. Mama wore a robin's-egg-blue silk cocktail dress and matching pillbox hat. My sister wore a fit-and-flare over-the-knee number with spray-painted Vans. I wore a flower crown and charcoal-gray wool.

Or as the Greek relatives reported, "The bride wore black!"

They saw this as a bad omen, but I didn't.

To me, a bad omen was a runaway groom.

I know a woman whose fiancé left her at the altar. I know a woman whose fiancé broke up with her via text message six hours before their rehearsal dinner. I know a woman whose fiancé broke it off the day they were putting their invitations in the mail. All three of these women cut their losses and married other men within a few years. And yes, unforeseen problems arose at those weddings, too. But they went through with their weddings.

Like my parents, my sister and I went through with our weddings.

Because bad stuff happens. And for better or for worse, how we handle such stuff on our wedding day predicts how well we'll handle such stuff—from duct tape to dental work, from traffic to tipsy toasters, from fainters to fires—from this day forward, until death do us part. Amen.

Matters of the Heart

When my first-generation Greek American husband left Manhattan to meet my parents for the first time in Alabama, he brought them a bottle of olive oil. Yes, this was before TSA confiscated breast milk and cough syrup. My husband carried a bottle onto a plane with the ease that a drum major leads a parade with a baton. The bottle was glass, the cap sealed with wax. The fancy grocery where he'd bought it had tied a ribbon around the neck.

Mama cooed and made a big to-do over the olive oil. She set it on the kitchen counter in a place of honor: by the Crock-Pot. When my husband returned two years later, he found his gift unopened and unmoved.

"Mrs. Ellis," he asked, "don't you like it?"

"Oh, I love it!" Mama said. She had dusted it like a lava lamp, but it had never occurred to her to use it.

Most southerners cook with butter. If we don't have four sticks of butter in the fridge, we don't have enough butter. Until I moved to New York City in 1992, I'd never heard of olive oil. If asked, I'd have guessed it was something you smeared on your face at night to prevent wrinkles. Or maybe it was a newfangled fuel for flying cars.

When I got married in 2001, I wanted to be a good wife. And being a good wife, to me, meant trying out the recipes my husband's Greek grandmother—whom he called "Yiayia"—used to make. I'd been raised with the mantra If you can read, you can cook. But like any beginning reader, I shouldn't have started with moussaka, the recipe equivalent of translating *War and Peace*.

Moussaka is like lasagna: there's ground beef and layers. But, instead of noodles, there are eggplants, which you have to disassemble, slicing them so thinly that they could be slid under a microscope lens. Take your eyes off them while they're under the broiler and they'll burn. Not to mention you have to make your own bread crumbs. Then there's béchamel. Béchamel, I'm pretty sure, is French for "carpal tunnel syndrome." Some people don't do windows, I don't do béchamel. But back then I gave it a whirl (or, more aptly, a thousand whisks) and presented my husband with a moussaka that was somehow rubbery and crispy with a dash of nutmeg as subtle as an NBA referee's whistle in church.

We are married now because he ate that then. And I have become a better cook because I've learned that, like a great marriage, a great recipe doesn't have to be a lot of work.

My specialty, *keftedakia,* are small Greek meatballs, garnished with lemon wedges and eaten without sauce. They are a far cry from what I grew up with: meatballs on top of Ragú on top of spaghetti, or the Swedish variety, simmered with a can of Campbell's cream of mushroom soup. Both are delicious by the way, but Greek meatballs are light and fluffy and include dill, oregano, and mint—which is basically a salad.

Olive oil is part of the Mediterranean diet, discovered by scientists in the 1950s and promoted by the American Medical Association because it reduces cholesterol and your chances of stroke. My husband's *yiayia* is proof: she lived to eighty-six. And Mama still can't get over how much more beautifully olive oil is packaged in comparison to butter. Plus, it does wonders for my cuticles. And as my husband reminds me, it's good for our hearts.

Nowadays, there is always an open bottle of olive oil in my kitchen because olive oil greased the gateway to my adventurous cooking (although my husband thinks I was always adventurous: until he met me, he'd never heard of ambrosia, which is sour cream mixed with marshmallows, shredded coconut, and pineapple tidbits). My husband says my *keftedakia* are better than his *yiayia*'s, and this makes me very proud of myself. I use her recipe from a worn stapled paperback Krinos Foods cookbook. But I'll admit that when I fry the little meatballs in olive oil, I throw in a pat of butter.

We Are Not That Couple

*I*nside a narrow restaurant off Madison Avenue, our friends Spiros and Rosalia waved to us from a table for two set for four. The old haunt was burgundy and brown, low lit and heavily mirrored. Windows fogged from heat rising off wall-to-wall diners. Fur coats slumped over chairs like sea lions at the Central Park Zoo.

We hugged because hugging was back in style, but Rosalia and I admitted that we were glad face-kissing seemed to be a thing of the past.

When the pandemic shut down New York City, Spiros had been up close and personal with the ventilated and the dead. He is chief of surgery at Bellevue, where he had stopped performing nonessential surgeries when his hospital was overrun with COVID-19 patients. Every day for months, he supervised a team of twenty to care for them. When he got home, he stripped in a section of his apartment—partitioned off by a shower curtain—and then showered in a bathroom used only by him to protect Rosalia and their daughters.

These safety precautions lasted a week.

"It was too depressing," said Rosalia. "I took the plastic down."

"And I never caught it," said Spiros. "Those N95 masks work. But," he added, "I was so dehydrated, I *did* get a kidney stone."

Rosalia ordered a plate of stuffed focaccia for the table. She is such a natural hostess, she makes you feel taken care of no matter where you are. Once at a Christmas party, she shaped a cheese log to look like a candy cane. My kind of hostess.

Spiros said, "I signed Rosalia and me up for a half-marathon."

"I don't run," said Rosalia.

"It's only a half-marathon, but the problem is it's on Greek Easter."

Rosalia said, "He thinks we are going to start training tomorrow and run a half-marathon in five months and then show up at our friends' house on Long Island that same day and eat a leg of lamb. But I told him, *We are not that couple.*"

"But I want us to *be* that couple!" said Spiros.

When it comes to activities, my husband and I are like horse-pill-size multivitamins: one a day. All my mara-

thons are on HGTV. I won't run to catch a bus. I burn
calories talking with my hands. And Greek Easter is a trip
because it's usually a week after *Easter* Easter, so we get all
that leftover candy on sale. I have never been as high as I
was twenty-two years ago at my husband's cousins' house
in Tivoli: jacked up on half-priced jelly beans and Robin
Eggs, pogo-sticking with one kid and then climbing a tree
with two others, hollering, "*Christos anesti!*" in my deep
southern accent, my mouth smeared with chocolate rabbit's carcass like Cujo with Cadbury rabies. Greek Easter
eggs are dyed red to represent the blood of Christ, and for
fun we butt ends to see which one cracks. I—an Alabama
native who grew up thinking Easter meant it was time to
bust out my white Buster Browns—would never have imag-
ined I'd be this into my husband's traditions. But marriage
is trying out and finding out what kind of couple you are.

Or aren't.

In our twenties in the 1990s, we took beginner swing
dance lessons because everybody in New York City was
taking beginner swing dance lessons because everyone
in New York City went to the movies (because that's what
couples did) and saw Vince Vaughn push his friend to "Go
Daddy-O" to Big Bad Voodoo Daddy. Turns out we are *not
that couple* who signs up for intermediate-level dance lessons. Flips and shoulder straddles are for ballroom com-
petitors. We are content to rock-step at weddings.

"And not go to weddings," my husband says.

On our first trip to New Orleans together, I had my tarot cards read while my future husband waited for me on the curb. He already knew that we were not going to be that couple who dabble in the occult, but I come from stock who lap it up like gumbo, so I told the tarot card reader to shuffle up and deal.

She laid out three cards and told me, "You are with a man who is mentally sick."

I said, "Do you mean I *was* with that man?"

"No," she said. "Leave *this* man, he will ruin your life."

I cried when I repeated what the psychic had said, but my future husband said, "Would you have believed her if she'd told you that you'd never be a writer?"

"No."

"So why do you believe her about me?"

I haven't seen a fortune teller since. And my husband, by just being his sweet self, has become my muse and given me four books of material.

In our thirties, we rented a villa with friends in the rolling grape-filled hills of Montepulciano, which is Italian for "the middle of nowhere," and we haven't put ourselves in such an isolated situation since because we are *not that couple* who wants to get away from it all.

My husband says, "It mostly all boils down to one thing: we don't drive. We're that couple who doesn't drive. So we don't like to go places we can't easily extract ourselves from."

No, we don't want to be your houseguests. We are *not*

that couple who wants to shower in your en suite or sleep on your sheets. (What is this, flannel?) We don't want to ignore whatever your dogs are doing. We don't want to play whatever game you think is fun to play but we think is aggressive. (What is this, slapjack?) We will come to visit you, but we will stay in a hotel.

My husband and I used to be that couple who never took the first room that a front desk clerk gave us. And by we, I mean me.

"Do you smell that?" I've asked him about what I've suspected to be fire, mildew, or blood. "Do you smell pennies? Is that burnt toast? Am I having a stroke?"

His answer is invariably, "No."

My husband used to tell people, "Helen will change hotel rooms three times before she's satisfied."

But he knew that I had our best interest at heart. So he'd put on a united front and park himself in the hotel lobby while I went up and down the elevator, sniffing out rooms and rejecting views of parking lots and—once at an Atlantic City Caesars—an interior view of a casino slot court. But once we hit our forties, I stopped testing his patience and started shelling out money for a guaranteed better room.

The longer we're together, the more admiration we have for couples we are not.

We're not Dani and Kevin, who make T-shirts and foam fingers to commemorate family activities. We're not my sister and her husband, Stefan, who every Halloween put on a show for trick-or-treaters (this year he was Jaws and she was Roy Scheider). We're not Bernard and Carmine, who like to eat supper at ten thirty at night *after* going to the theater. We're not Jean and Jim, who ride matching Harleys.

Jean said, "*We* are not that couple who agree to act our age and go gentle into that good night."

My friend Laura said, "I signed up for a monthly massage membership at the spa. Ed has a membership as well. The receptionist said we could do couple's massage. I told her Ed falls asleep and I can hear him snoring from across the room and then I can't stop laughing. *We* are not that couple who does couple's massage."

My friend Donna said, "*We* are not that couple who drives their kid around to play sports and spends every weekend at a Best Western."

On my sister's honeymoon in Hawaii, she and Stefan signed up for a kayak tour.

The tour guide said, "I need the member of each couple who's going to steer to sit in the back."

My sister sat in the back. Stefan, who'd never held a paddle, plopped down in the front with, as my sister describes it, "all his puppy-dog eagerness."

All the other men sat in the back.

The tour guide said to my sister, "The person *who steers* sits in the back."

"We're good," said my sister. But then she spent two

hours reminding Stefan, who was hypnotized by the beauty of Oahu, to paddle—"Paddle, Stefan!"—so that they wouldn't crash into the shoreline.

Since then—when asked if they want a two-person kayak (a question my husband and I have *never* been asked)—my sister and Stefan say, "We are not that couple" and choose one-person boats to go along and get along side by side.

Sometimes you try things out as a couple and find out that you are *not that couple,* but you are very much that person. My husband and I took chess lessons; now only he plays chess. We went to a crossword convention; now only I do the crossword. Bridge lessons: me. Bike riding: him. Brunch: me. Batting cages: him.

I told my friend Martin about our most recent marital activity over supper at Rolf's German restaurant, which is decorated with so many Christmas ornaments it feels like you're eating bratwurst inside Santa's sphincter. "Martin," I said, "you will never believe what we finally did after talking about it for all these years!"

Martin guessed: "You had a three-way?"

"No, we took a tennis lesson."

Heading into our fifties, my husband and I ask each other, "Are we that couple who play tennis?" We liked our lesson. I foresee a second. All we can do is try and find out.

Martin said, "I'd have guessed the three-way was more likely."

I said, "We are *not that couple.*"

A Woman Under the

Influence of

Joan Collins's *Dynasty*

$\mathcal{M}$y husband said, "You should stop binge-watching *Dynasty*. I'm afraid Alexis is going to be a bad influence on you."

We were eating supper—my husband sitting on the sofa with a plastic container of salad in his lap, and I was on the floor, eating tuna tartare off a coffee table like a toddler in a high chair, dragging french fries through a salt and pepper ketchup swamp. Onscreen, Joan Collins was eating blueberries with a silver spoon from a hollowed-out papaya in the solarium of her ex-husband's forty-eight-room mansion, which she'd just bought out from under him.

I said, "I want to be exactly like her."

Well, maybe not a thrice-divorcée with a caviar addiction (she once ate it straight out of a can in jail when she was standing trial for murder), but I want to live like a

1980s TV villainess (aka Alexis Carrington Colby, formerly Dexter).

If someone doesn't return my call, I want to climb into the back of a Rolls-Royce and flip through a *Vogue* as I'm chauffeured to their home or place of work. No, it doesn't matter if they're in bed or in a meeting. I will tuck my patent leather clutch under my armpit, barge in, and demand an answer.

If I don't like what I hear, I will slap that person across the face. I will slap a lady in a hospital. I will slap a lady in a hotel room. I will slap a lady in front of a shih tzu. I will push a lady down a mudslide. I will wrestle a lady in a koi pond.

I wasn't put on this earth to walk on eggshells. The world is my western omelet and everyone in it is diced ham.

I wear my heart on my sleeve like a grenade.

Business is business, so every week with no explanation whatsoever I will have a new young male assistant.

I'll say, "Thank you, Chad."

"It's Brad, ma'am."

"Yes, so it is," I'll say. And then I'll pull out a silver compact and reapply lipstick so red and so lacquered that his will to live gets stuck in the gloss.

I want to wear makeup so heavy it exceeds JetBlue's carry-on limit. I want to wear big hats and bigger wigs and, instead of a facelift, yank my natural hair back into a chignon. I want to wear suits so powerful they blow fuses like two hair dryers in one outlet. I want to wear silk negligees that cup my bosoms like ring bearer pillows. I want to wear evening gowns by Nolan Miller. Yes, feathers and sequins go together. And, yes, a neckline should plunge like Greg Louganis going for gold.

I want to redecorate our apartment with pastels: pink, purple, and peach with touches of teal. Yes, the headboard should match the drapes. Yes, the carpet should be so plush, if you drop your change purse, you can kiss seventy-nine cents goodbye. I want giant birds of paradise plants in gigantic woven baskets that throw more shade than I do. I want abstract art that's easier to appreciate than penicillin in a petri dish. I want to bathe in a round tub the size of a flying saucer and be taken away by Calgon bubbles up to my eyebrows.

I want to forgive the unforgivable: Alexis forgave her daughter for sleeping with her husband, her son for poisoning her son-in-law, and her ex-husband for strangling her. By season 8, they're all one big happy family again.

I want to live in a time when everything works out for the best. Everyone presumed dead is found alive and all kidnapped babies are returned. You can survive anything: car crashes, house fires, avalanches, oil rig explosions, oil rig explosions *at sea.* Blindness, amnesia, and paralysis aren't permanent medical conditions, they're just a case of nerves. Get over yourself! The only thing that kills you is incredible sex.

I want a sex drive that rivals a Chevrolet dealership. I want the devil-may-care confidence to get nekkid in broad daylight. I want to know that I'm the most desirable woman in the room, even if I'm the *only* woman in the room. Romance is in the eyes. Love is in the brain. There's no substitute for experience. Age is *most definitely* a number and fiftysomething beats a twentysomething by a lot.

Alexis says, "I enjoy my own company just as much as you enjoy it."

Alexis says, "Oh, I'm always right about everything."

Alexis says, "Given the right inspiration, anything's possible."

My husband should be thanking me for binge-watching 161 episodes and counting of Joan Collins's *Dynasty*. Who doesn't want to be under the influence of a woman like that?

Married . . . with Plants

*T*he first thing my friend Kay said as she stepped into my apartment after not seeing it for nineteen months was, "It's a jungle in here!"

When New York City began to shut down because of the pandemic, Kay had hightailed it out of town with her two Instagram-famous American shorthairs, Perry and Monty. An hour before she loaded her cats in her Mini Cooper, my husband walked me twenty blocks to her apartment, where along the way I bought a dozen of her favorite Linzer tarts from Greenberg's as a thank-you for her parting gift to us of an eight-pack of Northern quilted toilet paper.

I'd asked my husband, "Are these the last glimpses of civilization?"

He'd asked me, "Did you really ask your father to mail you a gun?"

On the walk home, businesses were boarding up their glass storefronts.

I'd asked my husband, "Who's going to loot Schweitzer linen?"

He'd asked me, "Did you really mean it when you said you'd break into our neighbors' apartments?"

By mid-March 2020, most of our neighbors were gone. Our super had told us that only thirteen out of sixty-two units were occupied, and I was sure that our dearly departed had left refrigerators, kitchen cabinets, and pantries of food. Not to mention hooch. If my husband and I ran out of provisions, I was not above dragging him from floor to floor, going door to door, picking locks and having picnics.

But it never came to this because grocery stores stayed open because grocery store workers came in to work.

Our neighbors settled into second houses or they rented second houses in Connecticut, Vermont, New Jersey, Rhode Island, the Bahamas (oh, yes, the Bahamas), and Maine. Maine was a big one. Who'd ever heard of Maine outside of a Stephen King novel? But flocks of our friends were in four-bedrooms by the sea, disinfecting lobster rolls and virtually schooling their kids.

In October 2020, they said they weren't coming back until January to avoid the Second Wave.

When the Second Wave hit, they stayed away longer.

Kay, for the most part, had been in *the country,* which to

me is anywhere outside of Manhattan or wherever there is an animal that won't curl up in my lap. Lockdown intensified *the country* situation. City mice became country mice, and animals *came out.* Deer roamed the streets. Alligators were extra *gatory.* Friends texted photos of bears in their backyards, sidling up to their birdbaths like sots at a bar. Kay texted photos of raccoons in her laundry room.

Outside our Upper East Side apartment windows, there were birds (or as I called them, "pigeons *plus*"). Cardinals, blue jays, and robins rested on our fire escape. With little to no traffic on the streets, we heard them sing when we woke up. Hawks and falcons were spotted in Central Park. I saw the notorious snowy owl.

Inside our apartment, we had cockroaches so big one crawled across my napping husband's forehead and woke him up.

He'd said, "I thought it was your finger, gently caressing me."

My husband couldn't go back to sleep until the orange cat and I had hunted the roach, flattened it with a shoe, and presented it to him on a paper towel like a trophy.

"It's not your fault," an exterminator told me. "You're not dirty, you're wet."

Turns out that with so many vacant apartments, roaches (or as New Yorkers call them, "water bugs") were leaving dry apartments all over the city and flooding up through drainpipes to get a drink. Our newfangled handwashing routine must have been a siren's call the likes of Maria Muldaur's "Midnight at the Oasis."

In September 2021, it was Puzzle Posse night, and four of the five of us—Dani, Megan, Kay, and I—were ready to pounce on a five-hundred-piece jigsaw of a beheaded priest under the stars. Our fifth member, Camille, was still in Maryland, where she and her wife had relocated at the start of the pandemic. Who knew when they'd come back? They had a puppy and a pool.

More than a year ago, Kay had said, "I'm not coming back to New York until I don't have to eat in the gutter."

Manhattan restaurants had reopened to indoor dining with proof of vaccination, so Kay was back, double-vaxxed, and unmasked with the rest of us.

So what had everyone been up to?

Kay had needlepointed sixty-three pillows. Dani had thrown her son a virtual bar mitzvah. Megan had written a novel about murderous ballerinas. I'd barbered (I can do a full military buzz cut on my husband in four minutes flat) and become a pandemic plant lady.

All my life, I've had a black thumb. When my husband rang my doorbell on our first date, I looked through my Bleecker Street peephole to see a rubber tree that he'd brought as a gift. I killed it. When I moved to Waverly Place, he brought me a jasmine plant and I killed it. When I moved in with him, someone sent us a ficus, which I promptly killed. *How* did I kill these plants? I do not know,

I just killed them. One day they were leafy, weeks later not so much.

Now our living room windows were blocked by a wall of monsteras, which spread from our orange recliner in one corner across ten feet of hardwood to our pewter couch in the other. Stalks reached into our living room. Catcher's mitt–sized leaves grew as high as our chins.

Dani gaped at the greenery. She said, "I'm used to seeing your Christmas tree in that spot, but this is something else."

Before the pandemic, the only hint of *the country* we'd ever had in our apartment were Christmas trees, which are really dead trees that you make look less dead by coating them with kitsch.

My husband and I switched to fake Christmas trees in 2010 when the orange cat (then a kitten) leapt into our last real tree at seven a.m. and brought it down like Dwayne "the Rock" Johnson would clothesline Timothée Chalamet. From our bedroom, I heard it fall. *Jingle, jingle, jingle* went the ornaments. Then *WHOMP!* I am telling you, seeing it KO'd like a prize fighter, I blacked out from rage. When I came to, I found my husband—stripped out of his work suit—diligently sweeping up the Shiny Brite carnage.

The orange cat had no interest in our fake flocked white tree because it smelled like plastic, because it was plastic (and the old cat has no interest in anything that's not tinseled in ham). In the off-season, we kept the tree dissected in two body bags in our basement storage cage. But after a few years, the fake white tree yellowed like a bad mall-Santa's beard, so we thanked it for its service and (like everyone in New York City does with their real trees) laid it to rest on the street with the garbage. And somebody took it because in New York City anything on a curb is fair game. When my husband and I redid our apartment, we laid his mother's chandelier on the curb and a woman—without breaking her stride—scooped her baby out of his stroller and slung our chandelier in. Unlike my family, my husband does not believe in garage sales. His motto is *He bought it, he breaks it, well he bought it so that's that.*

For the last five years, we've had a gold tree. The manufacturer calls the color "champagne," but it is as gold as a gold tooth and as gaudy as a stripper's thong. It's as understated as a disco ball in a manger. I like to flaunt it in our living room windows to décor war with the across-the-street neighbors. The neighbors who put trees in their windows don't know we're at war. But my Christmas tree stares into the souls of their Christmas trees and laughs like Vincent Price in the face of Raggedy Ann.

Megan asked, "When you put your Christmas tree up, where do the plants go?"

I said, "We move the plants."

Before I became a pandemic plant lady, I'd thought all plants could live without direct sunlight because on TV they lived without direct sunlight (Lord knows, I do). I'd been binge-watching Joan Collins's *Dynasty* and there were plants on vanities and mantels deep inside the Carrington mansion and on desks and by fax machines at Colbyco. But in July 2020 when my bamboo palm—which I'd placed behind a blue velvet swivel chair for, you know, *drama*—died, I realized that those *Dynasty* plants might have been as fake as the look-alike Sammy Jo hired to impersonate her aunt Krystle, whom she'd kidnapped and kept in a barn in season 6.

In February 2020, I'd bought that bamboo palm because I'd dreamed I'd bought a bamboo palm and sometimes if I can make a dream of mine come true, I'll do it. The six-foot palm arrived wrapped in a funnel of brown packing paper and sprang out like Debbie Reynolds from her *Singin' in the Rain* cake. I was giddy as I scooted it into the living room. When my husband got home from the office, *when* would he notice it? *What* would he say about it? I'd never made a purchase as impulsive as this. *Who* was he married to? I don't *do* houseplants.

But most southerners garden.

In 1940s Yazoo City, Mississippi, Mama's grandmother had a famous flower bed of orange and black-spotted hybrid tiger lilies. Next door, Mama's parents were always on their knees planting seeds. When Mama's mama campaigned for a mimosa tree, her "fastidious" husband fought the purchase because the tree looked like something Dr. Seuss dreamed up, with "Surrey with the Fringe on Top" pink puffs that made a mess and smelled too sweet to describe. But she got one anyway. And when her son (Mama's brother, *my* uncle Will) tried to climb the sapling only to split it in two, she tied a bedsheet around the trunk to save it despite her husband's protests that it looked like there was a mummified Ziegfeld girl in their front yard.

The next generation kept it simple. Mama had ferns. Uncle Will and Aunt Marguerite still have a concrete planter shaped like Jimmy Carter's grinning head. Papa never had a shrub he couldn't keep alive with a sprinkler.

"The front yard was okay," my sister remembered about our childhood home in Tuscaloosa, "but the backyard was a wasteland of dog doo, yellow grass, and tall weeds."

"Well," Mama explained, "sometimes you make choices in life."

When my sister turned thirty, she made the choice to have a half sleeve of magnolias, camellias, honeysuckles, and dogwood flowers tattooed on her arm to honor our southern heritage.

If life's a garden club, I'd never done anything to earn an honorable mention.

But then I had that dream about the bamboo palm. And I thought, *Should I give it a go? I'm older now. Maybe I'm more responsible. I've kept cats alive. There's no denying my attraction to straw hats with brims as wide as crop circles. I dig gloves and sharp objects.*

A New York City friend once said to me at an airport, "Helen, I didn't realize you were from Alabama."

I'd said, "Didn't you see me barefooting through the TSA?" I'd thought, *I don't mind dirt. Dirt washes off.*

So I bought that bamboo palm and kept it alive for a month. And no, my husband did not notice it until I introduced it to him like a plus-one. I was so proud of myself, I bought two more large plants based on the website searches "easy care" and "low light."

And then the world shut down because of COVID-19. And I wondered if my dream had been prophetic. You know: I'd have houseplants when pigs flew, hell froze over, or my husband started working from home. My husband thinks he manifested the pandemic because we RSVP'd to a karaoke party and he didn't want to karaoke. On March thirtieth, the party was canceled. My husband felt guilty but relieved. Until we were asked to karaoke a month later on Zoom.

In August 2020, I had a virtual plant care consultation with Alika Turner, aka Jade, aka The Black Plant Chick. I'd found her on Instagram because the app eavesdropped on my plant talk, especially words directed at my husband that went something like, "How could you not notice we have plants? We have plants. We have many plants."

Jade used to write and perform erotic fiction. She has a voice made for late-night radio call-in request shows and a beauty made for the big screen. She sat on the floor of her Atlanta home surrounded by plants, more in her element than Esther Williams surrounded by synchronized swimmers. From her side of our forty-five-minute FaceTime appointment, she directed me on how to hold my iPhone camera so that she could inspect my plants from all angles.

"Oh my goodness, look at those plant babies," she said. "What a good plant mama you are!"

I was so grateful for her reassurance, I teared up. Then I expressed my concerns about how I'd been winging it.

"No, no, no, you're good." She assured me that it was okay to have kept my plants in their nursery pots inside their decorative pots so that when I watered them, the water would run through the holes.

She said, "Plants need holes in their pots like we need holes in our faces."

"And other places," I said.

"Exactly," she said, laughing.

Until our "plant therapy" session, I hadn't known that I was supposed to water plants so much that the water ran out their drainage holes. I hadn't known I should rotate plants to distribute sunlight. I hadn't known I was supposed to spritz them and dust them, oil them and spike their water with fertilizer. Nor had I known that birds of paradise were meant to live in jungles not Manhattan apartments and it was normal for their leaves to curl and split so that wind could pass through.

"Just leave them be," Jade said, instantly forgiving me for having hacked off some of the leaves that I'd believed to be dead.

We made an appointment to talk about winter care, she wished me a blessed week, and she emailed a list of products that we'd discussed.

I bought nearly all of it: humidifiers, dipsticks, Miracle-Gro, pesticide, a squirt bottle, and moss poles for my monsteras to climb. I did not buy grow lights for the same reason I don't have picture lights clipped over my paintings: I find them pretentious.

My plants flourished. And watching them flourish, I flourished. And so I bought more plants.

I bought a snake plant, two ZZs, and a lemon lime. Two weeks later, I bought a fiddle-leaf fig. Two weeks after that, I bought calatheas—a Dottie and a pinstripe. Then pothos— one golden, one neon. Then a white butterfly and a strawberry cream. I bought a Birkin and learned that its roots are aerial and are *supposed* to grow above the soil. I forgave myself for burying them.

And then came the influx of caftans and planters.

What can I say? Cooped up in quarantine, my apartment turned into a sitcom, starring a sex-crazed housewife and her put-upon husband, or as I liked to call it, *"Three's Company and I'm Mrs. Roper."* Helen Roper never left her California apartment and she always looked as happy as a Clamato Bloody Mary, gadding about in her floor-length shapeless gowns, talking to herself. I mean, to her plants. I liked the way her apartment looked. All orange and yellow and green and brown. It felt *mellow,* man. And so I found myself on eBay searching "vintage mushroom planter pots." Mushrooms were the emojis of the 1970s. And folks were big on putting plants in animal sculptures. I bought a glazed lion that lives next to a wicker elephant in the Coral Lounge, and I am still on the hunt for the perfect brass swan.

I can admit now that I was addicted. I started sneaking plants into the apartment they way shopaholics sneak in shoes.

At one point, my husband asked me, "How many plants do we have?"

I asked, "How many do you *think* we have?"

He asked, "Eight?"

I said, "That sounds about right."

He asked, "How many do we really have?"

I shrugged. Correct answer: twenty-seven.

For my fiftieth birthday in October 2020, my husband took me to the botanical gardens in the Bronx for our first *nonessential* trip. My friend Patti sent me a ponytail palm. My friends Ann and Hannah emailed me a gift certificate and I ordered the most expensive plant the online retailer had to offer. Another friend brought me a mason jar of weed.

She said, "You can't get caught with this, it's so far above the legal limit in New York. Burp the lid twice a day, it's still curing." The ultimate pandemic plant lady, this friend had taken up farming marijuana in Vermont. Her 2020 harvest was Orange Sherbet; 2021 was Mother of All Buds.

In February 2021, I confessed to Jade in plant therapy that I had lost some of the plants in the cold season. And by *lost,* I meant murdered.

I smother-mothered my succulents. I sun-poisoned my calathea. I had to unsubscribe from a plant of the month club because the plants came in pots with no drainage holes and I gave them root rot. I *hurled* two philodendrons to their deaths when I slipped and fell watering my plant babies at the kitchen sink. And I don't know where the teeny tiny flying insects came from before they came out of my Silver Ripple, but they were everywhere and my husband and I spent our evenings clapping them to death. I couldn't cure the infestation, so the plant went in the garbage.

"It's okay to let plants go," Jade said. "Sometimes we just have *too many* plants."

Before my parents moved from Birmingham to Pasadena to live near my sister and their grandkids in July 2021, my sister and I threw them *The Last* Last Garage Sale, and the first things to go were Mama's plants and planters.

"Oh, your mother has such good taste," said so many Garage Sale People. "Is she still with us?"

"Yes," we said. "She's in the bedroom."

On *The Black Plant Chick* podcast, Jade said, "I want to encourage other people not just to let go of plants, but to let go of other things that you're holding on to. And make room for new things. Because a lot of time when God is trying to bless us, we tend to be holding on to things. And he's not going to give you something new if you can't let go of that old thing. And that can be relationships, that can be a job."

During the pandemic, my husband let go of a newsroom, his favorite part of being a journalist. And I'm sad to report that I let go of some friends. But the two of us have grown closer than ever.

We bought a second fake Christmas tree, which we put in the Coral Lounge away from the windows. This one is pink—it's just for us.

Slumber Party Side Effects

May Include . . .

When I was ten years old, I was hypnotized at a slumber party. All of us who were there are over fifty now, so none of us remember exactly how it started.

My friend Laurie said, "I know we were probably bored and looking for something to do after Truth or Dare. Was I dangling a pocket watch? I mean, I don't think I had a pocket watch."

My friend Vicki said, "You were on the floor, Helen, flat on your back. Laurie was sitting by your head and the rest of us were sitting around you."

Laurie said, "I'd been reading Dad's shrinky-dink books and the one I'd gotten a hold of was about hypnotherapy. Oh lord, Dad's going to kill me for this, but hey he's retired so what does he care? Anyway, I remember telling you that your arms and legs were getting heavy."

Vicki said, "Laurie started off by having you say funny

things, but at some point we all realized that you were answering as another person, maybe from a past life, or something like that. We were like, *Whaaaaat?* Then it got more serious trying to find out who was speaking from you. It feels like this went on for hours and hours. We were riveted and awestruck. Then Laurie regressed you back in age, and you were a child."

The other girls chanted, "Go back more, go back more."

"Then a toddler."

"Go back more, go back more."

Laurie said, "When I took you back to being a baby, you babbled. Because babies *do not talk*!"

The other girls chanted, "Go back more, go back more."

Vicki said, "And then there was silence. We freaked out and realized that you must be *in the womb*! There was this moment of fear and panic. *What do we do now?*"

Laurie said, "I think I wondered if you were faking, but you were convincing as hell."

Vicki said, "You deserved an Oscar."

My friend Paige said, "I slept through the whole thing."

Laurie asked me, "You weren't really hypnotized, right?"

Honestly, I've never been sure.

Back then, I was what Laurie's psychologist father would have called "susceptible." Meaning, I'd grab a Ouija board planchette faster than a TGI Fridays pager. If we played Light as a Feather, Stiff as a Board, I was the board. Kitchen table séance with a Magic 8 Ball? The answer is, *It is decid-edly so.* So why wouldn't I give my mind and body over to a sixth-grade hypnotherapist?

I remember being sprawled out in my sleeping bag, my eyes shut, my eyelids, my arms, and my legs getting heavy. I remember those moments when something in my brain clicked and I knew that babies babbled and fetuses don't do anything. I don't remember how I came out of the trance (nor does anyone else), but I remember the sun warming my face as it shone through a picture window and the heat of my friends' fear that they had gotten me stuck.

They'd seen me stuck before.

I was a notorious sleepwalker and nearly impossible to wake up.

My friend Mary Jo said, "Every sleepover at my house, you knocked over a Coke in your sleep."

Mary Jo and I lived three houses apart. The day my family moved into her neighborhood when I was seven, there was a knock on our front door and there stood six-year-old pigtailed Mary Jo.

She asked Papa, "You got any kids?"

Papa nodded and pushed me out into the yard.

I probably spent that very night at her house. And spilled a Coke. Or Dr Pepper, which is what her mama, Loretta, still drinks for breakfast every morning at ninety years old. Mary Jo's family became desensitized to me sleep-walking across their rust shag carpet like some parents accept that their kid's friend counts her Tater Tots before she eats them.

Mary Jo said, "I can still hear my dad say, 'If Helen Michelle is coming over, better buy extra paper towels.'"

By middle school, my friends had seen me sleepwalk and dump Legos in a toilet. They'd heard me talk nonsense or stare unblinkingly at them from my bed. On a Girl Scout spelunking overnight trip to Cumberland Caverns, Tennessee, I woke to the echo of a bunch of Brownies screaming in the pitch-black darkness as I dangled over the edge of a pit with a troop leader gripping the back of my T-shirt.

So whatever my friend Laurie did to me in Early 1980s Young Ladies Slumber Party Land was par for the Psych 101 course. Or witchcraft. This was Alabama. Yoga was witchcraft. "Eenie, meenie, miney, mo" was casting a spell. Origami paper fortune tellers predicted whom we'd marry and how many kids we'd have. Playing paranormal was as normal as frying canned biscuit doughboys for breakfast. We ate it all up. We liked being scared and we liked scaring one another.

We told ghost stories (don't say anybody's name in a mirror); told serial killer stories (it is *never* a tree branch scraping the roof of your car); and watched slasher films (it's not your dog licking your hand in the dark, *a man can lick as good as a dog*). We snuck into "off-limits" rooms

(I saw a "tastefully nude" black velvet portrait of a girl's parents over their waterbed); swiped stuff from medicine cabinets (I stole a green tube of Revlon Bamboo Bronze); and spied (I climbed out of a girl's first-floor window and watched through a neighboring window as her much older brother fooled around with his girlfriend on multiple dares. Is this why pricker bushes arouse me as an adult? Maybe so). If we chickened out, we told truths worthy of emotional blackmail. We chugged Mello Yello/Sprite suicides and sucked M&M's from the bottoms of Pepsi bottles to get higher than the Studio 54 cocaine moon and spoon. The lack of sleep drove us mad. But if you *did* fall asleep, you risked a Magic Marker mustache.

Laurie said, "That was unfortunate. But hey, it wore off after a few days, right?"

Several women I know stopped going to slumber parties because they were too uncomfortable with these antics topped off by the challenge of changing into pajamas. Some girls *arrived* in their pajamas, climbing out of station wagons in broad daylight because they couldn't master the contortionism it would later take to get out of their school clothes with a flannel Lanz floor-length floral nightgown slipped over their neck like a church revival tent. If challenged today, I can slide my bra out of my sleeve on the 6 train. But other girls let it all hang out like yoga witches air-drying at the YWCA. And to those of us who were so flat chested we could shimmy through a cat door, there was nothing more mesmerizing or shocking than your BFF's B cups.

"Oh my gosh," I remember a friend whispering about another's girl's breasts, "they're bigger than my mom's!"

At some point in the night, we'd turn our collective *Crucible*-like prowess on others. Stoked by *When a Stranger Calls* (the calls are *always* coming from inside the house), we made phony phone calls because in Early 1980s Young Ladies Slumber Party Land there was no *69 to catch us red-handed holding our touch-tones, FaceTime was *all the time* we didn't spend on a phone, and caller ID was what we called manners. As in, "Hello, this is Helen Michelle. May I please speak with Mary Jo?"

What was obscene was listening to boys we had crushes on stammer, "Hello? Is anybody there?"

We were the heavy breathers.

I called one boy's house so many times, when his mother picked up and heard my particular brand of eerie silence, she called out, "Dan, it's for you!"

But sometimes we girls went too far.

One friend led a year-long campaign to relentlessly crank-call a sixth-grade teacher. The teacher, a fragile lady with a Princess Di haircut who could have been in her twenties or fifties for all we knew, always picked up her phone. Weekend after weekend, after our parents had turned off their lights, and while we girls were trying on contraband lipstick, my friend would pick up one of our bedroom phones and call our teacher's home and pretend to be other students' mothers calling to complain. She pretended to be a pizza place demanding to know our teacher's correct address to deliver a hundred pizzas. She pretended to be a demon possessing the phone line. In one malicious stroke of genius, she pinched her nose and pretended to be a messenger from a made-up business she called the Compliment Delivery Service.

"This is the Compliment Delivery Service calling with a compliment for you from your third-period social studies class. The compliment is: You are as pretty as a picture"—she paused—"of shit."

I can still see the rest of us: mouths and eyes wide open in horror.

My friend handed me the phone and I heard our teacher cry.

This teacher quit. And as far as I know, she never taught again.

A few years later, some girls in my high school class pulled the same stunt with a soft-spoken young man straight out of teaching school. They harassed him on his home phone on weekend nights, but went further and enlisted their boyfriends to berate him in class. When *he* quit, our principal replaced him with a Vietnam veteran, who had a forearm tattoo of a snarling helmeted bulldog under which were inked the initials "USMC."

"Y'all know what these letters mean?" the battalion cap-tain asked our class.

"United States Marine Corps?" said some kid eager to be teacher's pet.

"No." The battalion captain sounded like he had a cigar in his mouth, but he most certainly did not. "It stands for Uncle Sam's Misguided Children."

We never called his house.

I'm not proud of myself for what we did when we were girls, but these things *did* happen. We made them happen.

And you had better not cry about it.

In Early 1980s Young Ladies Slumber Party Land if you cried once, you were labeled a crybaby for life. Just as if you wet the bed once, you were a bedwetter for life. If you called your parents to come and get you before the sun came up, you'd never live that down. Every slumber party was a test of character. Even if there was an act of God, you stuck it out.

Every Girl Scout camping trip I went on ended with a tornado and me clutching the ponchos of our two troop leaders like a wet stuffed animal pinned to a laundry line because Mama had told me, "Helen Michelle, if there is a tornado, you grab hold of those two big women. Those two big women will anchor you to the earth!"

All adults weren't protective.

In Early 1980s Young Ladies Slumber Party Land, some dads left their *Hustler* magazine collection where we could find it (a naked woman in a meat grinder will scar you for life). Still, this encouraged some of us to pose and take our own "dirty" pictures. A friend of mine who grew up in Detroit dropped rolls of such film off at a Fotomat kiosk, where employees developed the pictures, slipped them into envelopes with the negatives, and handed over what would now be reported to the authorities as child pornography.

"They didn't call our parents," my friend remembered. "Or ask us *who* took the photos."

All adults weren't safe.

I personally saw a friend's eighteen-year-old brother punch his fist through a door and another friend's father backhand her across the face. I woke to the silhouette of another girl's dad standing in a doorway studying us as we slept. When another friend's stepfather crawled into bed with us, I inched toward her headboard as he told X-rated fairy tales and inched his fingers up her leg into her pale-yellow nightgown. I told Mama all of this and she never let me sleep at these girls' houses again.

My slumber party days are far behind me, but the side effects linger.

If I was an Ambien-like drug marketed to my husband, my TV commercial voiceover would say, "If taken at bedtime, HELEN is good for fidelity and prolonged enthusiasm, but common slumber party side effects may include an inability to doze off with an arm or a leg hanging off the bed because *the devil might reach up and grab it;* double-checking the freezer to see if her bra is in there; wiggling her toes to see if she has sleep paralysis; a distrust of dust ruffles; trouble telling demon spawn and a hamper apart in the dark; a ringing in the ears that she will believe to be spyware; hyperawareness to noises that she will believe to be intruders; dreaming that there are rats under the covers, which she will make you search for until she fully wakes up; shrieking when you get back into bed after you pee; talking to you when you talk in your sleep; asking you questions—*that only you would know the answers to*—to see if you're a changeling; growling *back* at you just in case your snoring is not snoring, but a red flag that you're possessed—and whatever has possessed you needs to know that *she is not having it;* poking you if you're *too* quiet; pushing you to *get up and go see what the hell is going on out there;* a drop in your sex drive because she sometimes wears nightgowns straight out of *Little House on the Prairie;* and an inability to fall asleep without locking the bedroom door."

The lock on our bedroom door is the same kind I had on my bedroom door when I was a kid. There's a push button on the inside knob and on the outside knob is a tiny hole that you can slip a bobby pin into and pick. It's more for privacy than protection. I'm not going to install a deadbolt and chain because that would *really* be crazy. The sound of the push-button click is enough.

My husband has never asked me why I need to lock our bedroom door before I can close my eyes and sink into sleep. I wonder if he assumes it's simply a condition of *all* women. Left over from nights we spent together as girls. A phase hard to shake. A habit that stuck.

How to Keep House

$\mathcal{I}$f you don't know what's in the tinfoil, you don't want to know what's in the tinfoil. If you don't wash that cookie sheet, it will never leave your sink. If you smell your shirt to see if it's dirty, it's dirty. Don't question why the trash bag is so heavy, just throw it away.

Yes, you may toss a paper towel over that and deal with it later. Yes, it is perfectly fine to buy a new one instead of cleaning that one.

Say, "Hello dustpan, my old friend."

High five the drapes.

Slowclap your freezer. Junk your junk drawer. Find your potential between sofa cushions. Flirt with household accidents. Refold your bra drawer because it looks like a turtle orgy. Whatever that was has dried now, so scrape it up with a cheese knife.

Send the monster under your bed out to be dry-cleaned.

Windex your crystal ball. Wear a colander like a crown and march around with a spatula. Cut a sponge into a voodoo doll and do what you got to do to you know who. Build an igloo out of toilet paper rolls, crawl inside, and take a moment just for you.

Vacuum your feelings.

Angry cleaning is still cleaning. Drunk cleaning is still cleaning. Slow cleaning is still cleaning. If you can fold a fitted sheet, you can conquer the world.

How to Collect Art

*H*ere are things I've bought that are most definitely art: a bowling pin lamp; a vintage postcard of two Little Lord Fauntleroy–looking kids eating ambrosia; a portrait of a former employer (taken by his art school son) posed on a tennis court with his best friend, both shirtless in their swim trunks and clutching their cocker spaniels; a colored pencil drawing of an adult Wendy's fast food Wendy squatting on a cheeseburger; a needlepoint of eye surgery; mixed media of two monkeys smoking dope in front of a cabbage; fourteen midcentury paint-by-number clowns; and a watercolor of a rooster by a seventh grader. When a Jackson, Mississippi, middle school secretary found out I'd bid fifty dollars for that rooster in a PTA strip mall silent auction while in town for a family reunion, she called me in New York City to say she had another one just like it, would I like to buy it, too? I did.

And then I bought a rabbit head.

I found it in a public park in Alabama at the annual Kentuck Festival of the Arts, where for fifty years northern gallerists have chartered buses and come down to buy Gee's Bend quilts and Mose T paintings to resell at quadruple the price. Growing up, I was taken every year by my parents, who bought ceramic goblets and dragon sculptures. I used my allowance to paint my thumbprint into a cartoon mouse, layer colored sand in a jar to make a sunset in a jar, marbleize paper, and loom potholders.

Mama pointed at every artist's tent and said, "Oh, Helen Michelle, *you* can do *that.*" Solder jewelry, hand-blow glass, weave baskets, repurpose scrap metal into windmills. "Oh, Helen Michelle, *you* can do *that.*"

Taxidermy was not on her list.

The last time I went to Kentuck, I was forty-eight years old and bewitched by a rabbit head. The artist/taxidermist had mounted it on an employee-of-the-month-size plaque and surrounded it with moss. It had light brown fur with cotton-candy-pink marble eyes and a glittery gold unicorn horn hot-glued to its forehead. A woman working the Butch Anthony "Intertwangelism" yurt (google it, you won't be sorry) had already snatched up another rabbit head and proclaimed it to be the best, most undervalued work at the fair. The head I liked was $175 (including shipping).

"Get it!" my sister encouraged me. She'd already bought a mosaic key holder to nail on the wall by her kitchen door (over which hangs a screen print that reads, DON'T BE A JERK).

I asked, "You think it's good?"

"It's freaking awesome. Get it! And then tell me what your husband says when he sees what's in the box."

What's in the box? We all remember Brad Pitt asking Morgan Freeman at the end of the movie *Se7en.* Oh Brad, from my personal experience, the answer is not always "a head." But it was this time.

When my husband opened the UPS box and saw the rabbit head, he lost all color. He asked, "Is that thing real?" And then he asked, "Where are you going to hang it?"

I didn't answer because even though he didn't *say* he didn't like it, I *knew* he didn't like it because when people ask, "Where are you going to hang it?" what they mean is, *Is that art?* It's like when people say, "Look at that baby!" when they see an ugly baby. Or "Look at you!" when they see a friend who's made a poor plastic surgery decision. They can't say, "Nuh-uh!" because the mistake has already been made. I'd thought I'd bought a masterpiece, but my husband thought I'd paid hard-earned money for roadkill.

So I gifted the rabbit head to my friend Brianna, a former dominatrix whose most memorable client used to pay her to wear a latex nude bodysuit and stomp on Barbies and He-Man dolls because he liked the fantasy that she was a giant woman toy figurine. She did this barefoot because he liked to see her crush the dolls' heads between her toes. If she'd filmed herself doing this, I am quite sure the Whitney Biennial would show it on a loop in a little black room behind a black curtain.

Because here's what no one in the art world is telling you: museums are places curated by people who think they know what art is.

Here are things I've seen in museums: van Gogh's starry, starry night; Michelangelo's David; Matisse's goldfish; and Ferris Bueller's favorite dot painting. But I've also seen a woman in what looked to me to be a bathrobe sitting in a chair all day staring at people, including James Franco; two naked people in a doorway who were there for me to shimmy between (I slid my purse through first); portraits of a dude who ran a needle and thread through his face like a vintage Milton Bradley Embroidery for Little Hands fluffy yarn sewing card; a video of a woman holding up kitchen utensils alphabetically; a full-scale model of a kitchen with everything beaded (including a bag of Lay's potato chips); a full-scale model of a deli made out of felt (including bags of Lay's potato chips); a pile of candy; a rotary phone with a lobster glued to the receiver; a leg with a candle glued to its knee; a shark in formaldehyde; and a urinal on a pedestal.

Mama said of all of it, "Oh, Helen Michelle, *you* can do *that.*"

But why would I?

I want to be surrounded by art that makes me feel happy or sentimental or inspired or strong. And my husband wants art that doesn't make him feel frightened that whatever's in the frame will come to life and slink onto his chest while he sleeps.

When I moved into the apartment that my husband grew up in, it was filled with art that his Greek mother and grandmother had chosen. So, we're talking religious icons, large oil paintings of peasant women, leatherwork, and a sepia paperweight of my infant husband sprawled in the buff on a bearskin rug à la Burt Reynolds's *Playgirl* centerfold. My childhood home was filled with stuff passed down for centuries. So, we're talking frosted vases, large oil paintings of Civil War generals, daguerreotypes, and a chifforobe. When I moved from Alabama to New York City, I didn't take any of my family's art with me. After a few years of living with my husband, we gave most of his family's art to Greek relatives and all but one of the icons to a Queens cathedral, and he and I started our own art collection.

We have been collecting art for more than twenty years.

The first things we bought when he was a junior reporter and I was a secretary were museum posters—a forty-dollar frame around a fifteen-dollar memento was a chance to see a Picasso on our wall. When we made a little more money, we bought *prints,* which aren't as expensive as *originals* because there's more than one of them—think Andy Warhol soup cans, but what we've got is a screen print that is 1 of 150 of Alex Katz in a fedora. Then we bought *works on paper,* which means the artist painted on a sheet of paper instead of a canvas. I have no idea why our Holly Coulis painting of her cat jumping over a lemon is less expensive because it's on paper, but it's a fraction of what her canvases cost, so I don't ask questions.

We find a lot of art by going to art fairs, which are big spaces with a bunch of art. You pay an entrance fee and look around. Kentuck takes place outdoors, rain or shine, and artists sell their own work. In New York City, art fairs are held in piers, convention centers, warehouses, and emptied-out office floors—and gallerists sell their artists' work. The art is more expensive because there's a middleman and because it's New York City, but if you ask for a "collector's discount," they'll knock off 10 percent.

In New York City, fairs are broken down by category. "Folk art" means poor people did it and "outsider art" means crazy people did it. "Emerging" means the artist is just out of grad school and their stuff is between three and four figures. "Contemporary" means a piece of the artist's work is in a Midwest museum and costs ten figures. "Modern" means the artist has had major museum shows all to herself, so anything of hers you want will run you upwards of $500,000. "Fine art," forget about it. The artist is long dead and commemorated with coffee mugs. If you nick a frame with your program, your kids aren't going to college.

New York City is home to Sotheby's and Christie's, two of the biggest auction houses in the world. An auction house is a filthy rich person's garage sale, but instead of price stickers on the sides of clay ashtrays and souvenir seashell bands, an auction house publishes a full-color glossy program with pictures of some family's dead mother's Monet that they want to get rid of for $84.6 million.

But there are deals to be had.

From the Phillips auction house, we could afford a lesser-known Cindy Sherman print—Cindy dressed as a secretary at her typewriter—partially because it was one of an edition of 120 and partially because no one else bid on it. To this day I regret not buying a four-hundred-dollar stone squirrel doorstopper from Brooke Astor's estate auction at Sotheby's. And I regret not asking my Classic Trashy Book Club to go in on one of Jackie Collins's cocktail rings at Bonhams so that each of us could take turns wearing it for special occasions. I didn't do either because I was too self-conscious to admit what I liked.

Don't let the art world intimidate you.

Here's how you know what's art: you see it and you *don't*

ask yourself, "Where are you going to hang it?" You see it and you get that feeling that you feel at an animal shelter when you sit in a cat room with a lot of cats and someone picks up a cat and you scream at that stranger, "That's MY cat! Put down MY cat!" And maybe *your* cat ain't something they'd put behind Plexiglas at the Louvre, but there's more to life than *Mona Lisa*s.

Art is everywhere.

My husband and I have bought art off the street. We have bought art off the walls of diners and hair salons. I found a smiley face my husband finger-painted in the first grade and framed it. At one of our parties, my sister took a Polaroid of my friend Hannah with a lampshade on her head, and I framed it. And—in what has gone down in our personal history as the Best Houseguest Gift Ever—our friends Tony and Lynn took a picture of our cats, took that picture to a Central Park color chalk artist who immortalized them on construction paper, and you had better believe that I framed it.

And here's another thing no one in the art world is telling you: just because you frame it doesn't mean it has to stay on your wall until you die.

Papa likes to say, "Your mother only puts art on a wall if there's already a nail there."

My husband and I have a lot of holes in our walls. We've hired professionals to spackle and repaint the walls, but then we buy more art. We move or remove the art we have, and then there are more holes. And you know what, that's okay. It's holes in our walls, not holes in our earlobes. Art isn't permanent. You should enjoy it for as long as you enjoy it.

Some things are not on display in our home anymore. The bowling pin lamp, paint-by-numbers clowns, and museum prints were donated to thrift stores. My old boss and adult Wendy are in our basement storage cage. The eye surgery, seventh-grade roosters, first-grade smiley face, *Hannah with Lampshade,* and the Best Houseguest Gift Ever are stacked like LPs in our linen closet.

For a well-known nonhoarder, I'm embarrassed to admit there is a lot of art in our closets. I need to figure out what to do with it. Our friend Liz, an art consultant, surveyed all that we have and found only two pieces that she could resell because so much of our art isn't worth anything to anyone in the art world.

Why?

Because they say so.

But here's what no one in the art world is telling you: art isn't an investment, it's an experience.

Or like Mama always said: *You* can do *that.*

My husband and I have a tradition on Valentine's Day night: we stay home, we eat fondue, and we make each other valentines. I don't know when this started with us, but at some point early on, I got the idea and my husband embraced it. After all, would he rather plan an extravagant night out or sit at our dining room table, hunch over news-paper, and get down with a glue stick?

Our crafting has gone way beyond construction paper and crayons. One year, we painted rocks. One year we spray-painted a stool. One year, we papier-mâchéd bal-loons, let them dry overnight, popped those balloons, and watercolored the husks. One year, we made a paper chain that is now coiled in a Kentuck ceramic bowl in our liv-ing room. On each link is written something that we love about each other or our lives. A black Sharpie and strips of blank paper sit beside the bowl so we can keep adding links. The most recent reads, "Our old cat's breath." That old cat's breath is so awful, but we love it because it is just so, so awful.

As with collecting art, we've had some hits and misses with creating our own.

My husband said, "The collage years were hard because cutting out all those letters from magazines made me feel like I was making ransom notes. And then there was the décolletage."

I asked, "Do you mean decoupage?"

"What's the difference?"

"Décolletage is French for my nipples to my neck. Decoupage means paste. As in, 'I've entered my anti-aging serum years so every night I decoupage my décolletage.'"

When Valentine's Day fell during the Delta variant surge, my husband and I had extra time and pushed ourselves creatively. For weeks, I logged on to eBay and bought vintage classroom Valentines. I bought Simpsons cards from the 1980s with Ralph offering a picture of a train that reads, "I Choo-Choo-Choose You!" And from the 1960s through 1990s, I got Yogi Bear and Boo-Boo, Bert and Ernie, Ren and Stimpy, Tweety and Sylvester, the Pink Panther, Snoopy, Scooby-Doo, and Superwoman.

My husband and I spread hundreds of cards across our dining room table and stuffed four or five into small white business envelopes for friends. We mailed them off secret-admirer style. No signature, no return address. On the back flaps of the envelopes we wrote, #GuessWho Valentines.

Some friends guessed it was us by our handwriting. Some friends outside New York guessed it was us by the postmark because we are the only people they know in New York. Some friends posted the cards on Instagram and used the hashtag. Some friends who knew those friends wrote in the comments, "I got these too!" And some friends didn't pursue the mystery and just appreciated the art.

When Omicron hit, we transformed the Coral Lounge pink Christmas tree into a Valentine's tree. Off came the ornaments and on went our leftover class cards and years of homemade creations.

My husband said, "This was so easy, and our best project yet."

See, art is for everyone. *You* can do *that*.

Teacher's Pet

use stickers to commemorate our sex life.

It started eight years ago when I bought my first Lilly Pulitzer agenda. The calendar comes with two sheets of stickers, which along with fireworks to mark the Fourth of July and a champagne bottle to mark New Year's Eve, for some reason includes oranges, lemons, and limes. What are these for? I do not know. So, when my husband and I have sex, I stick a citrus on the date like a gold star as if to say, *A++! You deserve extra credit!*

"Did you see your sticker?" I'll ask him. "Do you want to put your sticker in my book?"

I leave my Lilly Pulitzer laid open on my desk—which is right next to our bed—the way an exhibitionist hides her diary under a paper clip. Stickers are encouraging. Stickers are addictive. Stickers are seals of approval. Once you get one sticker, you want another sticker. It's like why you want a lot of stamps in your passport and a lot of patches on your Girl Scout sash: you want to show off.

I give out actual gold stars when we host book parties at our apartment. I invite an independent bookseller to sell books and when a guest buys a book, I stick a gold star on her blouse. If she buys more than one book, she gets more than one gold star.

"Terri is a five-star general!" I'll brag to the room.

People in the publishing business think you should give away books *for free* at book parties because selling them is tacky, but I don't agree. If you're invited to a book party, it's because your friend wrote a book. Friends of friends who write books should buy their friend's book. Not buying a book at a book party is like going to a proctologist's wedding and expecting her, as she walks down the aisle, to give you and everyone else on the bride's side the finger.

So I'm pushy. I say to a guest, "You don't want to meet the author's parents without a gold star, do you? Don't you want to be like Terri? I see you, Terri, eating my home-made Chex Mix off your big ol' stack of books! Teacher's pet! Teacher's pet!"

Everyone wants to be teacher's pet. Anyone who says differently is lying to you.

I was an A student (I sat in front rows, I raised my hand), but never teacher's pet. Teacher's pet was class monitor when the teacher stepped into the hall. Teacher's pet handed out pop quizzes. Teacher's pet emptied the pencil sharpener that was bolted to the doorframe next to the American flag. Teacher's pet led the buddy system out of the building when there was a bomb threat. You got to be teacher's pet when you did something extraordinary like didn't squirm during lice checks.

A girl named Angel was our third-grade teacher's pet. With a name like that, I think her mother gave birth gunning for her to be teacher's pet straight out of the stirrups. As did the mothers of Tiffany, Taffy, Candy, and Penny Dollar, whose brother's name was Bill. With names like these, you're going to be treated special or shunned.

Angel and I ran neck and neck for first place in our third-grade reading challenge. Our teacher made construction paper kites with all her students' names on them and taped them to the "harmony" green cinder block walls. For every book we read, she wrote the title and the author on a construction paper bow and taped it to the kite string. At the end of the school year, whoever had the most bows won. The only thing better than a sticker is a bow. A bow flutters. A bow is a sticker with pizzazz.

I read library books with Newbery Medals because I was and continue to be a sucker for a book with a sticker stuck on it. I can spot a foil National Book Award or Oprah's O from twenty paces, and as an adult, I secretly long for a book that I've written to earn a famous sticker. When my last book was published, my friend Hannah made me some stickers that read, "Grown-Ass Lady," which make me feel very special because *I am* a grown-ass lady *who writes* for grown-ass ladies and for readers who *appreciate* grown-ass ladies. If you attended one of my two 2021 in-person events at Books Are Magic in Brooklyn or Magic City Books in Tulsa, I offered you a sticker. And you took it. Everybody took those stickers. It was like I was giving out Pfizer scratch-and-sniff vaccines.

Angel won the third-grade reading challenge, but I contested the win because she'd read Snoopy books. Her bows read, *Schulz, Schulz, Schulz, Schulz . . .*

I shouted, "Cartoon books shouldn't count!"

"A book is a book," my teacher told me. She taught me right then and there that book snobs aren't teacher's pets.

The best decision I made six months into the pandemic was to upgrade my 2020 Lilly Pulitzer to a *jumbo,* which is the largest of three sizes. My jumbo is spiral bound, broken up by week, and when opened, spans the space of a desk blotter. Lilly Pulitzer agendas start in August instead of January because they're intended for academic years. And I am here for it. Back-to-school time is the best time of year because back-to-school time is a time of reinvention and another chance to be teacher's pet.

The summer before tenth grade, I quit chewing my hair by getting a perm *and* a style as close to Flock of Seagulls short as Mama's beauty parlor would allow. I quit biting my nails with the help of something toxic that I painted on my cuticles. I went shopping with Mama, who—against her better judgment—bought me an outfit in a drab color best described as *olive,* which in the Benetton-bright 1980s was like topping her teenage daughter off with a funeral veil. But I felt New Wave and improved. The coolest kid in school agreed. I have a very clear memory of this Duran Duran–looking sophomore eyeing me up and down and saying something to the effect of, "You know, Helen, you're not so *emotionally out of control* anymore."

Emotionally out of control is not what he said. It's how Webster's dictionary defines the word he used that has since been canceled. When an *emotionally out of control* kid like me was passionate about something, she raised her voice, put on voices, talked in circles, and ran around a room. She didn't hold back. She shouted things like, "Cartoon books shouldn't count!"

My husband said, "I don't believe you were ever *emotionally out of control.* You're an elegant lady."

We were alone in our apartment and in all honesty I looked over my shoulder to see who he was talking to. I'm the lady who does "the pajama dance" (more Mick Jagger than Mata Hari) for him every night. I'm the lady whom my friend Ann's children call "the *loud* one." My friend in Florida's children call me "the *weird* one." New Yorkers mutter, "You're *cheerful.*" Which I've interpreted to mean, "It's six a.m. at LaGuardia, lady. Take it down a notch."

Don't get me wrong, I'm okay with this part of my personality now. It's just not who I wanted to be in high school. I wanted to be teacher's pet.

Teacher's pet was *put together* and *had it together*—and both traits could be judged by her back-to-school supplies. Teacher's pet had a three-ring binder with a clip-in pencil pouch, a four-color ballpoint, and a drawing compass sharp enough to pick litter up off the highway. Teacher's pet had a vinyl Pocket Day-Timer or a flat-flip wall calendar with monthly scenes of hot air balloons. Teacher's pet color-coded each subject's syllabus and shrank her handwriting to fit the day's space. She knew everything we were supposed to have done and everything we were scheduled to do.

Teacher asked, "What chapters were assigned for last weekend?"

Teacher's pet: "Four through eight."

"And when are book reports expected?"

"Two Fridays from now."

My school supply game always started out strong, but by homecoming I looked like I was carrying two books and a bird's nest. My locker looked like the inside of a scarecrow. Trapper Keepers were too complicated for me to use and too expensive for me to ruin.

When I was a senior in college, I thought I'd finally become teacher's pet. A creative writing professor praised my work in front of the class and encouraged me to write a novel for my thesis. But then he shut his office door every time I entered, laughed at me when I opened it, and laughed harder when I insisted the door remain open for the duration of our meetings. He repeatedly called me at home—at night and on weekends, suggestive and lewd—and laughed at me when I hung up the phone. During my thesis defense, he accused me of copying his writing style and not having an original thought of my own but quit laughing when an Italian professor—a woman I had never met, but who'd been brought in as a committee member—bellowed at him, "That's ridiculous! You're ridiculous!"

Looking back, he must have had a bad reputation on campus and she must have known about it. Or maybe she'd known enough men like him to recognize a predator with a thorn in his paw. As I do now. But when I was twenty-one, my teacher scared me. And I stopped wanting to be anyone's pet.

When my husband's regular Monday night poker game moved online because of the pandemic, they invited me to play. Whenever I booked a win, I marked it in my jumbo Lilly Pulitzer with leftover book party gold stars. For months, my pages were filled with constellations. Seeing them, I felt as high as the sky.

I kept the high going by marking small accomplishments with what Lilly Pulitzer stickers I had left. Call my parents, I gave myself a flower sticker. Cook supper, I gave myself a heart sticker. Walk, flip-flop sticker. Write, an *oh so meta* miniature Lilly Pulitzer agenda sticker. For my mammogram, I used a string bikini sticker that I'm pretty sure was meant for spring break. I kept using citrus for sex until I ran out.

So, I got creative.

At a drugstore, I found a sheet of red sparkly lips to mark our one-on-ones. The company that sells my favorite puzzles also sells stickers, so I bought a book of B. Kliban's black and grey striped cats doing yoga to mark when I exercise, and a book of Edward Gorey's fainting socialites for PMS days. I found a book of one thousand antiquarian ladies and gentlemen, bats and owls, skulls and feathers, and ornate letters that I use to represent and spell out the most mundane of activities like entering my tax receipts. And then I typed "vintage teacher rewards" into my computer and tumbled down memory lane.

There on eBay were all the stickers from the 1970s and 1980s that I wanted my teachers to stick on my homework when I was a kid. A cookie that says, "Smart Cookie!" and a possum that says, "Nothing's impossumable!" Kermit the Frog waving his arms and saying, "Hooray!" and Miss Piggy clasping her opera gloves and saying, "Good for *vous*!" And yes, gosh darn it, I discovered that the Peanuts gang knows exactly what I need to hear. Snoopy says, "Neat job!" Charlie Brown says, "Well done!" Linus says, "Great!" And Sally says, "Wow!"

Angel, if you're out there, please accept my apology for

judging your third-grade reading preferences. Schulz is a literary genius. *Schulz! Schulz! Schulz! Schulz!*

Like Charles Schulz himself, comic strip characters from the 1970s and 1980s weren't always happy. And neither am I. So I bought Cathy in her closet screaming, "Aack!" And Ziggy with his head in his hands lamenting, "Nobody understands me."

Who are these vendors who sell out-of-print stickers? I don't want to know. Where do they get their Care Bears, Smurfs, and Precious Moments? Not my concern. They dig up what's been lying dormant in a drawer for decades, jack up the price, and I pay it. On average four bucks for a sheet of six to fifteen. I have a ten-pocket folder with labels to organize them.

When I showed a group of friends on a Zoom call my obsession, one woman snarked, "I wish I had *all the time in the world* to play with stickers."

Her words stung. My cheeks and neck burned. I felt so stupid, so childish, so humiliated, so *emotionally out of control.* I had shared something so private that was giving me so much pleasure, such a tiny practice that was lifting my spirits in such an uncertain time, and for whatever reason, a friend had shut me down. I'm sure she didn't think twice about what she said, but it just about broke me.

I wanted to shout, "It takes less than a minute to stick a sticker on a day!"

But instead, I shut my mouth. I almost shut my laptop.

When our Zoom ended, I flipped through my Lilly Pulitzer to see if I'd been wasting my time.

I smiled at a sticker of the *Schitt's Creek* daughter going, "EW, COVID!" I smiled at a sticker I'd earned waiting in line for five hours that reads, "I voted early." I teared up with gratitude for our military and medical professionals when I saw a sticker that reads, "I got my vaccination at the Javits Center." I ran my fingers over Garfield, who marks the day our vet (clad in goggles, mask, face shield, latex gloves, and disposable shoe booties) made a house call to save our old cat's life. Every month is scattered with red lips and gold stars. And thanks to Edward Gorey, I see that bad moods pass.

In April 2021, I notice my stickers change the week I attended the burial of my friend Lori, who was a member of my Classic Trashy Book Club. Lori was pretty, wide-eyed, eager to laugh, and eager to believe. She really was a woman who lit up a room. She lit up our world. On the day we said goodbye to her, the sun was so bright we all went home pink.

When I got home, I covered the pages surrounding her death with butterflies, frogs, flowers, insects, and angels. The stickers overlap and make the open book look like a garden. I remember the peace I found in the process of creating something lush to honor my friend. Part meditation, part art. My stickers helped me cope.

They give me hope.

Some nights my husband will find me with my Lilly Pulitzer laid open on our bed, stickers spread out all over our sheets. I'm picking and choosing, peeling and placing. I haven't been at it that long, maybe an hour.

Without looking up, I'll say, "I'll be with you in a little bit, I'm doing my stickers."

Or sometimes, I *will* look up and ask, "Do *you* want a sticker?"

No matter his answer, there's no limit to my rewards. I can have as many stickers as I want. Go ahead and judge me. I am my own teacher's pet.

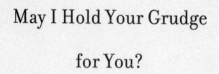

May I Hold Your Grudge

for You?

At a book party thrown for me outside of the city, a woman introduced herself as the wife of a man whose name she knew I would know. She was friendly and I think expected me to be equally friendly, but her husband was the ex-husband of a friend of mine whom I hadn't seen in twenty years, but to whom I'd remained viciously loyal. This woman standing in front of me was not the person he'd committed adultery with, but she might as well have been. I could not believe this man had thought that I'd forgiven him and that it was a good idea to send his second wife to an event with my picture on the invitation and tell her to waltz right up to me and tell me who she was. It took everything I had not to push her into a cut-glass bowl of pimento cheese to teach *him* a lesson.

Hadn't he learned anything fifteen years ago when he himself had come up to me and my husband in a one-room French restaurant in the East Sixties and said, "Hi, Helen!"

I swelled up like a cobra.

My husband shook his head as if to say to him, *Keep walking.*

"What?" said the ex-husband.

My husband said, "Hey man, trust me, you don't want to hear whatever she's going to say."

The last time a man I held a grudge against approached me in public, I'd introduced him as "the son of a bitch who hurt my sister."

Call me Karma's Little Helper. I believe in *What goes around, comes around,* but I'll take an opportunity to remind a person who's hurt a person I love that whatever they've got coming is coming their way.

I've said, "You know what you did."

I've said, "You're gonna get it."

I am born from generations of grudge holders. My family identifies people by what they did wrong. There's the kid who stuck his finger in my sister's Big Bird birthday cake. There's the kid who pooped in our playhouse and blamed it on our dog. There's the kid who convinced my sister to lie to my parents about sleeping over at her house, when they were really at a party. There's the kid who sucked my boyfriend's finger. Right in front of me. In our living room. On our good couch.

Now that my sister is a mother, she holds grudges against

kids who hurt *her* kids. She said, "There was this one little girl who was such an *asshat* to one of mine in elementary school that on the way back from a field trip, I stepped on her heel and said, 'Oh, I'm so sorry!' and then high-fived *my* child."

Mama raised us with a concept of do-it-yourself vigilantism that is rooted in her genealogy like a centuries-old oak.

Case in point: In the 1880s, a young French woman with a baby traveled by boat to New Orleans, then up the Mississippi River, to where Mama's side of the family lived in Yazoo City. She knocked on the door of a nearby house belonging to the Hill family claiming that their son had impregnated her while he was in medical school in Paris. The Hill family denied this and cast her and her baby out. To survive, the young French woman took up sewing for a woman in my family, Margaret Baker Harrison. Mrs. Harrison held a grudge against the Hill family for treating the young mother so badly.

Mrs. Harrison told her, "Tell me your story while you're sewing and I'll write it, and we'll publish a book."

When the book was published under the initials L. C. H.— a first run of a few thousand copies out of Philadelphia—the Hill family, who held a grudge against the young French woman and Mrs. Harrison for typesetting their dirty laundry, found every copy and burned them.

Mama tells me that only two copies of *Laure; or, the*

Blighted Life survived. I have one of them. Along with a ring with Mrs. Harrison's initials, which I wear because I too am a woman who holds grudges.

I've heard that holding a grudge is like swallowing poison and expecting the other person to die. But holding a grudge for a friend is no more taxing than holding her lipstick or set of keys in your purse. Or holding her bottle of poison so she won't be tempted to take a sip. It's a matter of loyalty. It's a way of saying, *That person was wrong. You will always be right to feel the way that you do. I'm on your side and I will forever be on your side. And when that person gets theirs, we will rejoice.* It's called "being a good friend."

If a friend forgets why you hold a grudge for her, you should remind her. If a friend knows why another friend holds a grudge *against you,* she should tell you.

My friend Dani asked a friend, "Does Sally not like me for some reason? And if so, why?"

Her friend said, "What Sally thinks of you is none of your business."

Now Dani and I hold a grudge against the friend who said that.

Mama says, "There's a difference between holding a grudge and *hating* someone. You can *socialize* with people you hold grudges against."

This is true. If you introduce yourself to me at a party and I say, "Oh, I know who you are," what I mean is, *You hurt my friend, nice to meet you, but you're dead to me.*

It's not unusual for me to recognize a partygoer and then turn to my friend and ask, "Remind me why we hate her?"

If my friend can't remember, I let the grudge go.

My friend Ann says she holds three grudges for her friend Stacey but can only remember two. Stacey is not a bridge burner, but Ann implores her to stop reaching out to the women who hurt her. Every December, she says to Stacey, "Don't send those women holiday cards!"

Another friend has made me promise to hold a grudge against her husband if she dies before him and he remarries.

"Banish him," she said. "He never gets to have fun without me."

In my marriage, my husband is the Great Letter-Goer. When I see him forgive and forget, he might as well be levitating. The man releases personal affronts like a magician frees doves from his hat center stage. My husband does not believe in *What goes around, comes around.* He does not believe that there is a greater force in the universe interested in evening your score. Or your friend's score.

He says, "Life's too short to have a shit list."

But I love my shit list. If I had the nerve to type it, I'd laminate it. It's like a mental to-do list. More realistically, it's a three-drawer, army-green, sharp-edged metal cabinet full of folders. Every time someone gets what's coming to them, I get an endorphin rush from pulling their file and making a mark on their permanent record.

The last time someone wronged my husband, I said to everyone we knew, "Oh, he's on my shit list. If I see him in public, I will *tell* him he's on my shit list. I'm tempted to kick that son of a bitch and run."

My husband said, "Helen, your anger isn't helping me."

His comment stopped me cold. Wait, what did he mean? That couldn't be right. My anger, my grudge, my shit list were expressions of my love. They meant, *That person was wrong. I'm on your side and I will forever be on your side.* I'd thought I was being a good wife. But I wasn't. So, for my husband, I turned my anger off.

I kept my grudge—and all my grudges ever after—to myself because sometimes *just the thought* of what you'd do to someone for someone you love is payback enough.

So, when that woman waltzed right up to me at that book party and told me she was married to the ex-husband of my friend, whom I hadn't seen in twenty years, but to whom I'd remained viciously loyal, I shook the lady's hand, signed her book, and thanked her for coming.

On the way home, I said to my husband, "Did you notice I didn't say anything bad? Did you notice I didn't do anything bad?"

"Yes, I did," he said. "Good job."

My friend Todd has a theory he calls "Todd's Law of Averages." He says, "When someone wrongs you, don't do anything. It may take a week, it may take a year, it may take twenty years, but that person will get theirs."

It took five years for the man who wronged my husband to get what he deserved, and I found out what had happened to him because my friend Koula emailed me a news article detailing his fate. Koula and I used to work together as secretaries and—long after I left the job—we remain a team.

I clutched my iPhone with her email like she'd sent me flowers, a heart-shaped box of chocolates, and a bottle of wine. "You remembered!" I wrote back to her. "I'm so touched that you remembered."

Two nights later, we met in a multiroom French restaurant in the West Fifties and I thanked my good friend for holding a grudge for me.

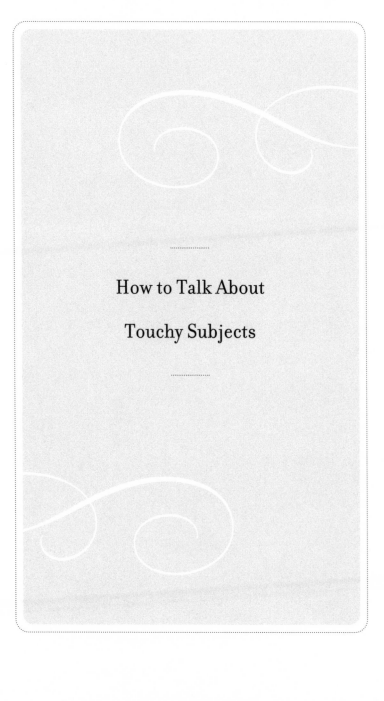

How to Talk About

Touchy Subjects

*M*y friend Charlotte likes to spring sensitive information on her fourteen- and twelve-year-old sons when her boys are facing forward, seat-belted, and captive in a moving car. For example, driving them to soccer camp, Charlotte said, "Just so you know, boys *and girls* masturbate. Boys masturbate with their penis and girls masturbate with their clitoris. Masturbating is normal."

From the back seat, her younger son said, "I feel sick."

"Because of what I said?" asked Charlotte.

"I don't know. I get carsick. I can't tell if it's carsickness or what you said. Please stop talking."

In the front passenger seat, her older son nodded in agreement.

Charlotte offers up such unsolicited but rational infor-mation because she believes in raising her sons with a non-shame-based sexuality. She doesn't want them learning about sex on the internet. Why? Because what they'll find there will make them think sex is so weird it should not exist on this planet. Google "vampire squid pineapple position" why don't you and see what I mean.

Charlotte has since revised her method of communication. She said to her boys, "From now on, if you have a question you're too embarrassed to ask me, I want you to write that question on a piece of paper and give it to me. You can fold the paper if you want to. Then *I'll* google it and write down the answer and give it to you."

I asked her, "Have they passed you any notes yet?"

"Not yet," said Charlotte.

"Maybe you need to make a Sex Ed Suggestion Box," I said. "You know, paint and glitter a shoebox and cut a slit in the top. You can leave it on the toilet tank so there's some level of anonymity."

My sister and I were raised with the notion that anything we wanted to know we could learn from a book. I learned about front-clip bras and "Ralph" in a highlighted, dog-eared paperback of Judy Blume's *Forever* that was passed under desks at Alberta Elementary School, but my sister sailed through prepubescence on a tide of confidence that she already knew it all.

At seven years old, she held up a green pea at supper and announced, "My baby is *this* big."

She'd thought all girls were born with a baby inside

them and as they got older, the baby got bigger, and when they got married, the baby was born. Papa and I shot each other a look and excused ourselves from the round daisy-yellow rattan table to leave it to Mama to explain the facts of life.

Years later at that very same table, I was sixteen and studying for the SATs and overheard Papa say to Mama, "If you have a moment, I'd like to talk with you about our sex life."

And no, I have no idea what specifics he wanted to talk with her about. My prolonged screaming that shut their conversation down echoes in my ears to this day.

When my husband and I were both twenty-seven and celebrating our two-year dating anniversary (yes, *dating* anniversaries should be a thing), he said in the courtyard of a West Village restaurant, "I want to talk with you about doing something you've said you'd never do."

"Whale watch?" I asked.

"No," he said. "Move in together without being married."

My parents call this tactic "the Red Lobster Approach." If they had news they wanted to lay on my sister and me when we were kids, information they wanted to get out of us, or something they wanted us to agree to, they'd take us to Red Lobster, the finest dining establishment in Tuscaloosa. As soon as we saw those lobsters in tanks at the hostess podium, our defenses were shot. They might as well have been kittens in cubbyholes. Our hearts bled all the way to a dimly lit pleather banquette. We shrank under shadows of two-foot-tall menus. One fried shrimp platter later, we were too stuffed to make a scene. Red Lobster's tartar sauce is a truth serum. We gave in to our parents' wishes or spilled our guts. And then we wet-napped the memory until we were tricked again. And again.

At some point as an adult, I built up a tolerance to the Red Lobster Approach and the wrecks-n-effects of rich food. I can eat a bathtub of risotto and confess to nothing more than my name, age, and Social Security number. And I have never been one to think that I owed a man anything more than a verbal thank-you when he paid for my meal.

My husband and I did not move in together until we were engaged.

As of August 25, 2022, my husband and I have been together for 9,862 days. Yes, that is the exact number, including leap years. How do I know? My husband calculates and writes the number on a note card once a year. See, I told you dating anniversaries should be a thing. Math is hot. And so is my husband. Especially when he presses pause on the remote when I bring up touchy subjects over *CBS Sunday Morning*.

CBS Sunday Morning is geared toward baby boomers, but we Gen Xers watch it too. The show knows what we want and how to give it to us: five minutes of complete and utter devastation, ten minutes on how getting older sucks, and an hour forty of not-dead-yet Woodstock musicians and their eccentricities. You know how Jane Pauley grips a rolled-up sheet of typing paper and goes, "*Today* on *CBS Sunday Morning:* Thousands evacuate Afghanistan as the Taliban violently seizes control, Ted Koppel asks why nobody's vaccinated in Mayberry, and Joan Baez has a new hobby: buttons!" (Insert trumpet sound: *Bah-dah-bah-dah-BAH-dah-DAH!*)

"Pause," I will say.

And my husband will press pause, then gaze over our two cats stretched like orange and licorice taffy between us to where I sit on the opposite end of the sofa in the Coral Lounge.

I'll ask, "If we had to flee New York City, how would we do it?"

I'll ask, "Am I right that your grandmother was a mail-order bride?"

I'll ask, "How often did you see your father beat your mother?"

And then we will talk about how his grandmother fled Smyrna in the Greco-Turkish War when she was a child, or the measures she took as an adult to move to America with her infant daughter to better her life, or what my husband's father did to his mother, his grandmother's daughter, when my husband was a boy in this very room where we sit.

All our married friends have different ways of communicating.

One pair takes nightly walks. The husband told me, "Sometimes we walk for ten minutes and don't say a word, but *I've told her* that I'm happy just to walk beside her in silence."

Another pair makes light of challenges that may lie ahead. The wife told me, "*I told him:* If you get fired, I don't want to know about it. You need to be one of those men who leaves the apartment and sits on a park bench and feeds the pigeons eight hours a day."

Another pair tells each other about a problem after it's solved. "*He told me:* I quit my job, but I have a new one."

Grandmother said that if she and Granddaddy couldn't settle an argument, they'd get all dressed up, go out to eat at a candlelit restaurant, and recite the alphabet.

Like, she'd say, "A, B, C, D."

And he'd say, "E, F, G."

They literally faked it until they made up.

This year, as COVID-19 restrictions were loosened in the city, my husband came home from a night out with the boys—and by boys, I mean middle-aged men. He said, "I have news."

I guessed: "The so-and-sos are getting divorced."

"What? I didn't even have the chance to give you any clues. How'd you know?"

I said, "Too many happy Instagram posts."

Since joining Instagram, I have muted at least twenty people I am friendly with because I don't want to see

how good they have it or how good they want to make me
think they have it. I don't want to see their vacations, their
second homes, their swimming pools, their hotel infin-
ity pools, their first-class airplane seats, their selfies in
beach chairs, Adirondack chairs, T-bars, and balconies.
And I especially don't want to see it during a worldwide
pandemic.

A friend said to me about a recent windfall, "I'm so
lucky and grateful, but I feel so guilty."

I told her, "All you have to do is keep it to yourself."

Here's what social media is for: *Golden Girls* clips and
cats. Not dead cats. I don't want to see a picture of your cat
in the prime of her life with a caption underneath that tells
me your cat is dead. If your cat doesn't appear in your feed
for six squares, I'll figure it out.

I still live by the Southern Lady Code: *If you don't have
something nice to say, say something not so nice in a nice way.*
For example: "Your Instagram is beautifully curated" is
Southern Lady Code for "Your real life must be a hotter
mess than spaghetti and meatballs in a clothes dryer." But
I would never write such a message in your comments. My
thoughts on your business are not the world's business.

To talk about our friends' public lives that we think
should remain private, a friend and I invented the Egg
Salad Method. When we *see* something, we *say* something.
Well, we *text* something. And that something is "egg salad,"
which means "Can you believe it?" We chose a code that is

innocuous and hard to figure out, unlike "code blue" in a hospital or "Redrum" in *The Shining.* For more on the Egg Salad Method, I offer you *eggs*-hibit A.

Me: Egg. Salad!!!

Her: Tell~

Me: Looooook yooouuu know whereeee!

Her: Well of course she does and of course she did and of course she is.

Her: Omg

Her: She's like that person who thinks she's the only person who ever ____

That's verbatim from a text exchange, including the ____, which I can't fill in because my friend actually typed out the ____ because she didn't want evidence of her quip in print. I honestly don't remember what went in the ____. But I do know I called my friend and filled in the ____ right after she texted me and then continued our conversation in glorious uncensored gory detail.

Because I'm Beetlejuice. Text me three times in a row and I will appear. I'll call you. Just try me. Go on, text me three times and see what happens.

Hang-Ups

$\mathcal{I}$n the fall of 2021, our friends Maxine and Peggy each dropped off note cards with our doormen. These women had never met each other, but both were over the age of eighty and worried sick. In immaculate cursive, both women had written, "What's happened to you? Your phone line has been disconnected!"

My husband had had our home phone number for his entire life. For the past twenty-some years, he and I had answered our calls to this number on two vintage phones. Yes, I am aware that *vintage* now includes the 1990s, but I am not talking about a cordless Sony the shape and weight of an empty box of Philadelphia cream cheese; a Tinkertoy of a telephone; a shrinking violet of a telephone you had to replant in its charger to keep its batteries alive; a shell you lost weekly in a couch. And yes, I am aware that this kind of phone had caller ID, but caller ID is for cowards.

Every time I see someone studying a phone like a nutritionist reads the back of a bag of Flamin' Hot Cheetos, I think, *Be a man, why don't ya, and answer a call without knowing who the heck it is.* And by "man," I mean a 1970s model with sideburns and a sensitivity chip on his shoulder who smokes while he shaves and dresses in a sports coat, velour V-neck, or head-to-toe denim.

Think Johnny Fever. Think Dirty Harry. Think Jim Rockford.

One of our landlines was a black push-button phone straight off *The Rockford Files.* We bought it on eBay because we grew up watching James Garner answer that phone. Neither one of us had seen this actor as an old man in *The Notebook* (and at this point in our lives, I doubt we ever will), but his middle-aged voice on his answering machine as detective Jim Rockford was *so cool,* and it made his phone *so cool* that his phone got a close-up before the coolest theme song ever composed kicked in.

Our other phone was a white lacquered metal rotary from the 1960s that weighed five pounds and sat on my white lacquered desk, right next to our bed. It loomed like every other phone you've seen on TV or in the movies made before 1995—its only plot purpose to ring like a bell *that tolls for thee* and let the main character know that someone has died in some ungodly way at some ungodly hour of the night.

I slept soundly because my AT&T clunker was my *home-*

made home security system. We all have them: do-it-yourself MacGyver ideas. Inklings that if push comes to shove our spy amnesia will clear up and we'll instinctively remember how to gouge a guy's eyes out. I know women who sleep with knives in their lotion baskets or baseball bats under their beds. I know women with panic buttons. Mama didn't have a panic button, she had a gun. But in New York City, people don't have guns stockpiled in their apartments like cans of Crisco. So as an adult, I've had my rotary. One bash to the skull and I'd debilitate an intruder before I hog-tied him with the mile-long curly cord and dialed 911.

Mama raised my sister and me to call 911 like some parents raise their kids to play the piano. Practice, practice. You never know when you'll find yourself in a situation to show off this skill.

Mama said, "Helen Michelle, when you dial 911, you state your name and your address before you say what your emergency is because if the emergency worsens and you're cut off, the police will at least know where to go to help you."

Once I said, "Mama, they can *trace* calls."

"Helen Michelle, do you know how long it takes to trace a call?"

"No."

"Well, neither do I, but I *do* know it takes *some* time and in that time you could be dead."

When my husband used his cell phone to call *me* (not 911) from where he was stuck in our elevator, I ran downstairs to the lobby to discover that the doormen had called the *super* (not 911), and so *I* called 911 and said, "This is Helen Ellis at such-and-such address. My husband is trapped in an elevator that is *yo-yoing* between floors."

I didn't hang up until I heard sirens. Five firemen strode into our lobby with an ax, a crowbar, and some sort of elevator skeleton key that shut down the ride and spit my husband out.

And please take a moment to learn this: if someone falls ill in your apartment, after you call 911, call your lobby and tell them to get the freight elevator ready. EMT stretchers won't fit into narrow-front passenger elevators. In the time it takes to get a staff member to unlock the freight elevator to get to your floor, your sweet someone could be dead.

Our telephone number was one digit different from what I gathered to be a geriatric specialist of some kind. His patients' voices were cracked like mausoleum paint and they were never the least bit impressed with my pleasant phone demeanor.

Me: "Hello."

Them: "Is this Doctor So-and-so's office?"

Me: "No, I am so sorry, you have the wrong number."

Them: "Is this 734-___8?"

Me: "No ma'am, this is 734-___0."

Click.

They hung up as if them calling me was my fault. Or they thought I was outright lying to them. Why? I guess for the same reason they think Burger King cashiers shortchange them: for sport? Nine out of ten times, they promptly called my wrong number again.

Me: "Hello."

Click.

Mama raised me to be so polite to wrong numbers that I called this doctor's patients back to tell them that they mistakenly left messages about their sciatica or what they suspected to be gout on my answering machine.

Me: "Hello, I just wanted to let you know that you left a message for your doctor on my home answering machine."

Click.

I don't blame them for their rudeness. I must sound like some scammer out to win their trust and then get them to fork over their FreshDirect password. My husband and I used to get calls like this every day because—since our landline hadn't changed in fifty years—scammers think we're at least seventy-five. Senile and lonely. And *boy oh boy,* do they go for the jugular.

Me: "Hello."

Them: "Gramma?"

Me: "You have the wrong number, please don't call here again."

I gave up being polite to unsolicited callers when one

shouted, "Oh, *madam,* I will call you *every* day! *A thousand times* a day!"

I once went out with a guy who told a mutual friend, "My motto is, once a woman doesn't return my *twenty-third* phone call, I know it's over."

I don't remember if I went on more than one date with this guy, what this guy's name was, or what he even looked like, but I do remember the twenty-three calls because I kept a tally on a pad by my answering machine.

Papa used to take great pleasure in teaching my high school suitors a lesson by way of our kitchen yellow wall phone.

Ring!

"Hello," Papa said like Bob Newhart at the start of *The Bob Newhart Show.*

High school suitor: "Is Helen there?"

"Yes."

And then Papa would slurp up the delicious silence, his ear to the receiver, rocking from heels to toes until the boy figured out that he should ask, "May I speak to her please?"

When my sister got to be a teenager and boys asked, "Is Elizabeth there?" Papa would say, "Yes." Wait a beat. And then hang up the phone.

I grew up admiring portrayals of women who made their livings with phones. Annie Potts in *Ghostbusters* ("We got one!"); Jane Fonda in *9 to 5* ("Judy Bernly, please hold.

Judy Bernly, please hold. This is Judy Bernly."). And it was not lost on me that Loni Anderson was the highest-paid employee at WKRP in Cincinnati. I believed that if you could manage three or more phone lines, you would always have a job. And, as a secretary for most of my working life, I always did.

Me: "Mr. So-and-so's office."

Them: "Is he in?"

Me: "I'm so sorry, he's unavailable. May I take a message?"

My boss was never *out of the office, in a meeting, with someone,* or *in the restroom.* They weren't standing right in front of me, shaking their head: *I'm not here.* They were *unavailable.* And to get to them, you had to get through a twentysomething, then thirtysomething, well-mannered, tight-lipped gatekeeper. It was a powerful feeling to be a guard, like my father was for me.

Years ago, our friend Dylan pointed out our home rotary phone to his then tween daughters and asked them, "Do you think this is from the past or the future?"

The girls had no idea. They took turns sticking their little fingers into the rotary holes with the wariness of sticking their little fingers into a bowling ball or a seat belt crack in the back of a cab. Then they took selfies making an old-fashioned phone call like I might pose at Dollywood blowing "Jolene" into a jug.

I don't envy younger women who have to fall in love

without a phone. I mean a *vintage* phone, sitting pretty in a corner, formal and squat like a sorority housemother or a book of etiquette. I grew up with rules.

Nice guys call you in advance for a date. Nice guys call you at a decent hour. The longer a nice guy talks to you on the phone, the more interested he is in getting to know you. You can tell a lot about a man by the tone of his voice. You can tell a lot about how you feel about a man when you recognize his voice when he says, "It's me."

My husband called me the morning after our first date. He called me so early, I was still in bed. I remember reaching over my clock radio to pick up my Slimline. I don't remember the color of my phone or what we talked about, but I remember being happy to hear from him.

I thought, *This a nice surprise.*

An hour later, I thought, *This is a nice guy.*

As we talked, tethered to our apartment walls, tethered to each other, I stared at the sun streaming through the blinds of my fire escape window. Back then when someone called you, you sat still and looked at what was in front of you. You listened. You talked and you listened. And the other person did the same.

When my friend Brettne learned that our landline was disconnected, she said, "I don't understand. The rotary phone is your whole *identity*!"

She suggested I make a purse to carry around one of

my leftover phones. She texted me a picture of a "purse phone," which is a tote bag with a square cut out for the push buttons and a hole cut out for the cord so that you can plug it into a phone jack.

"It's art!" she said.

"It is!" I said.

"So what happened?" she asked.

"AT&T broke up with us," I said.

When they first started calling, I'd thought they were crank calls.

AT&T: "Effective August tenth, 2021, we will no longer offer residential local service in New York and your home phone service will be discontinued."

Me: *Click.*

"They're bluffing," I told my husband.

My husband called AT&T, whose business had become so inept that they told him there was no record of our phone number. He said, "Well, *someone's* been billing us." Then he called our cable TV provider, Spectrum, which offered to convert our landline to an internet phone.

"What's an internet phone?" he asked.

Answer: we'd get to keep our number, which would be part of our cable box, and our bill would go from ninety dollars a month to fourteen."

"Fine," my husband said.

Three weeks later, Spectrum called my husband's cell

to say our landline had been disconnected—therefore they couldn't transfer the number. Despite our efforts, AT&T had pulled the plug. Our lifeline was lost.

Spectrum offered to create a new number for us, but it wouldn't connect to our rotaries, so where was the fun in that?

"I don't want another phone number," I said.

"Me either," my husband said.

I'm trying to list the pros of letting our vintage phones go.

1. We can cut the cords that creep along the baseboards, up the walls, across picture moldings, throughout the apartment.
2. The old cat won't wake us up by knocking the receivers off the hooks to create "the Howler Tone" when he wants to be fed.

That's all I've got so far, just two reasons to get rid of what I know we'll never use again. But I can't bring myself to throw our phones away. So I've placed the white lacquered rotary and private-eye push-button among our potted plants like statues in a garden. Aphrodite and Adonis. Unplugged, but still connected. Stone cold lovers, forever cool.

The Bright Side

$\mathcal{M}$y husband got a prescription for Viagra three months into lockdown. The pandemic was upon us and so we thought we'd take the opportunity to be *upon* each other. A little more than usual. In a new and improved way. I mean, why not? We had the time. We'd been monogamous for twenty-five years. We have two cats that sleep eighteen hours a day, no kids, and both of us were working from home, so what else were we going to do? Take a MasterClass on how to play the spoons or claw our way to the top of a pyramid scheme hocking hamburger-print yoga pants? I don't think so.

Before Viagra, our sex life had been very enjoyable. We love each other and we love sex with each other, but love is accepting changes and challenges.

A friend put it best about sex with her fifty-year-old husband: "Cold pizza is still pizza."

But hot sex ain't all about what the pizza delivery guy is packing. It takes two to tantric. And like the proverbial roller coaster, we've had our ups and downs.

When my husband and I were younger, we did it in a movie theater, the hallway of a friend's apartment, and a Paris museum. *Oh là là!* Now we do it in beds. Our bed and hotel beds. We don't spend long weekends in people's guest rooms, so our bed and hotel beds are the only beds we do it in. And those beds are plenty. Because beds are comfortable. We have no interest in cars because they're cramped, kitchen islands because they're cold, showers because they're slippery, and airplane johns because they always smell like seat 32C took a jalapeño popper dump.

For my bridal shower, the theme was lingerie and sex toys. Ten of my girlfriends sat around my living room eating coffee cake while I opened gift-wrapped vibrators. I got a pink Rabbit and a blue waterproof Bullet that was meant to be played with like a tub sub. I got a Hallmark card with a cock ring inside. I got a red teddy and crotchless panties. And then we played a game in which two women were blindfolded, and one woman held a roll of toilet paper between her knees, and another woman held a broomstick between *her* knees and tried to penetrate the Charmin.

And, no, Mama was not in attendance. But my sister, Elizabeth, was.

I have no memory of what Elizabeth gave me, so I'll say she gave me a throwback gift certificate to Spencer's (the

most risqué adult novelty store in our hometown of Tuscaloosa), which was the reason we high school girls went to
the mall in the 1980s to begin with. That, and to get a big
iced cookie and grip arcade joysticks. Blitzed on Orange
Julius, giggling like a pack of wind-up chatter teeth, we'd
sidle into Spencer's and read *Jokes for the John*.

Reading still turns me on, but I'm over Regency
romance novels where heroines' bodices are ripped in
haystacks and barns. I've also had it with TV directors who
keep filming women getting "made love to" against walls.
The latest trend is filming women receiving cunnilingus
against those walls, and against trees, and standing up
against their shoe shelves in their well-lit walk-in closets.
Every time I see such an act, I can't believe it's on basic
cable. And I can't believe it's satisfying. A clitoris is not as
accessible as a penis. Leading men look like they're trying
to lick a light switch through a neck pillow.

The bridal shower edible underwear was a one and
done. Same with the fuzzy handcuffs and *Kama Sutra* dice.
The blue vibrator rusted, the lingerie itched, and the cock
ring suffered the fate of all lost ponytail holders.

We never replaced any of it.

Because my slutty cheerleader days are a thing of the
past. Banana splits are for kids. If I do a herkie jump, I'll
risk a groin pull. My idea of kink is doing it with the laptop
charger light on.

My husband is fine with all this because what turns him

on is me. I will assure you the feeling is mutual. He's got bedroom eyes, smells like musk and mosquito repellent—hey, it's some mix of Barbasol and Vaseline for Men, and I like it—and his penis is my *third* favorite part of his body. So when it wasn't all that it used to be, I didn't mind because neither was I.

Wasn't it enough that we still wanted to be naked and affectionate?

My husband brought up Viagra to me a year before the pandemic but hadn't asked his doctor about it because his seventysomething-year-old male doctor had retired and the doctor whom his retired doctor had referred him to was a seventysomething-year-old woman. He didn't want to ask about Viagra during their first appointment because he said it would have been like him, as a schoolboy, asking his Greek grandmother to pack him a lunch box stuffed with spanakopita and a blow-up doll.

I found him a new doctor. Male, middle-aged, in-network, walking distance from our apartment, who was seeing new patients live and in person during a pandemic. Before my husband got home from his appointment, the CVS Pharmacy automated caller called and told me that his prescription was ready for pickup in a tone reminiscent of *Hello, and welcome to Moviefone!*

"For a list of sexual positions by genre, press one!"

A secret to a happy marriage is to seek out the bright

side. In June 2020, the bright side was fluorescent lighting behind a makeshift COVID-proof pharmacy bubble made from aisle 9 shower curtains and aisle 5 duct tape. Inside the bubble were pharmacists with pills. My husband handed over his insurance card and a pharmacist in a hazmat suit handed him a plastic bottle of sildenafil, a generic form of Viagra.

When he got home, he swallowed a pill.

How can I put this? I haven't seen *Star Wars* since the 1970s, but I know enough to recognize a lightsaber in my hand.

My husband asked, "Do you remember what it used to be like? Like, is my penis the same as it was in our twenties?"

"No. It's better," I said. "I feel like I'm cheating, but I'm not cheating. It's a brand-new penis."

"Except now I know what to do with it," he said.

He sure does.

My husband recovered on the sofa in the Coral Lounge. During lockdown—as we hung out the room's windows and cheered for essential workers—a passerby left a Post-it note with our doormen asking for the name of the paint color on our walls. As serendipity (and Sherwin-Williams) would have it, the answer is: "Rejuvenate."

But my husband looked depleted. He held a bag of frozen peas over his eyes to soothe a sinus headache, which is one of the sildenafil side effects, which also include a stuffy nose, dizziness, upset stomach, and trouble telling blue and green colors apart.

My husband remembers me regarding him with great sympathy and saying, "Oh no, does this mean that from now on every time that we have sex, you're going to feel awful afterward?"

After what we'd just experienced, he knew the answer was *yes*.

Another reason we'd resisted Viagra had been the fear that once we tried it, we'd never do it without it. Well, we were right. We ain't never going back.

You don't go back to a pogo stick once you've been hot-rodding. And no, I'm not sure of what I speak. My husband and I don't drive. But he can revel in the thrill of not stalling. And I can imagine what it feels like to fly down a desert highway with my head and arms hanging out a window, squealing in complete abandon. Because I did this in our bed, so much so I injured my neck with my overenthusiasm. I could not look to the right for a week.

My husband regarded me with great sympathy when he said my name and I had to turn my whole body.

"The next time," I told him, "try half a pill."

He did. It worked. No side effects unless you count multiple orgasms.

Sex on Viagra is so good, I have a recurring dream that I'm riding a subway and petting a dachshund. A wiener dog in a tunnel. I mean, how phallic can you get? To this day, if my husband shakes that pill bottle like a box of Tic Tacs, I have a Pavlovian response: my head pops up like the *Caddyshack* gopher from wherever I am in our apartment, and I make a beeline.

If someone told me when I was younger that the best sex I'd ever have would be in my fifties with my fiftysomething-year-old husband, I'd never have believed them. Because you see so few middle-aged married couples make love on TV. And none of my long-married friends will admit that their husbands take Viagra. A lot of my long-married friends tell me that they barely do it at all anymore.

Well, let me be the one to tell you: my husband and I don't do it every night, but we do it more than we've done it in years. Try as we might, we can't keep up with the prescription. But the CVS pharmacists keep calling with refills. And we walk the two city blocks, hand in hand, to pick up the pills from the bright side.

Permanent Vacation Plans

My friend Jean's son is an EMT and says the most common calls they get are LOLGBs: Little Old Ladies Go Boom.

But it's never the fall that kills them. It's life after the fall.

A friend found his grandmother collapsed in her apartment and called 911. After extreme lifesaving measures, his grandmother spent the next seven years as a vegetable. He said, "If I'd gotten to her place a few minutes later, she'd have died a happy woman."

When my husband's *yiayia* fell outside Grand Central Station and broke her hip, her health declined so severely that she Scotch-taped a Do Not Resuscitate order over her twin bed. Yiayia had made her decision and gotten it in writing. If EMTs arrived to find her life in jeopardy, they would see that sign and know what to do: nothing.

Mama is eighty-one and has given our family explicit instructions: "If something happens to me, wait thirty minutes before you call an ambulance."

I've said, "You mean call after I quit yelling, 'That's not the right light, Mama! Quit crawling toward the laundry room!'"

Not every family jokes about how they want to go out, but my family does. If we didn't talk about what we don't want to talk about, we'd never talk about what we don't want to talk about. We're not afraid of death, we're afraid of dying. Because dying can last a long time, hurt like hell, and be humiliating. So we joke about controlling what's out of our control.

On a father-daughter trip to Biloxi to play poker, over a breakfast of cathead biscuits and gravy, I confessed to Papa that I'd always thought he and Mama would die in a murder-suicide. Mama would get a terminal illness, and Papa would shoot her and then shoot himself. I'd get a call from a sheriff or neighbor, book a flight, and bury them.

Papa said, "Well, you're right, I don't want to live without your mother. But if she dies, I won't shoot myself, I'll take an overdose of insulin."

And I said, "Okay, pass the Tabasco sauce."

My parents are so serious about not losing their quality of life that they have living wills and have made me their official plug-puller. I have no problem with taking my parents off life support, but my sister worries I may be too quick on the draw. She foresees me arriving for a deathbed visit, yanking the first plug I see out of its socket, and her screaming, "Helen Michelle, that's not Mama, that's the air conditioner!"

Since I was a child, Papa has told me, "Don't ask me to kill you because I love you so much I'll do it."

His method: smother me with a pillow.

A lot of my friends have plug-pullers and pillow people. Two of my friends have the same plug-puller. Two of my friends have entrusted their deaths to a best friend instead of their husbands because they don't think their husbands will be strong enough to kill them before their bodies fail and trap their minds. Or it's the opposite: they think their husbands will let them go too easily.

My friend Paige's husband is a veterinarian. She said, "All he does all day is take fishhooks out of dogs' mouths and euthanize cats."

Another friend's mother told her, "If I get Alzheimer's, put me in the dirtiest most rundown nursing home you can find."

My friend asked her, "To save money? Because you won't know the difference?"

"No," said her mother. "So I'll catch a staph infection and die faster."

Another friend said to me, "I know I have to write this down, but I'm telling you that I don't want to reach a point where I'm incapacitated. I don't think my sister could kill me."

I volunteered.

My friend said, "Just so we're clear, a cane is okay. Don't kill me if I have to walk with a cane."

I regularly tell my husband, "If I'm dead, don't bring me back. No CPR. I've had a great run. I have no regrets. Just let me go. Because if you don't, I'll adjust to whatever happens to me. It's like when our dishwasher quit working two years ago at the start of the pandemic, and we still haven't replaced it because we've *adjusted* to using the busted one as a drying rack."

"We've adjusted to the stink," said my husband.

"*I know.* I keep changing out the baking soda and squatting on the floor with a turkey baster to suck out the mildew where water pools at the bottom. If *you* let me get to a certain point, you'll be sucking stuff out of *me.* Don't let me be the dishwasher."

"So what do I do?"

"Call Papa. Or take me to Oregon and give me *the shot.*"

"What if I can't do that?"

"Then dress me nice like Sunny von Bülow. Bed jacket and satin slippers. Have my nails done. Hire some gorgeous male orderly/massage therapist to dote on me and then stick his head out of my room every night at six thirty and say to you, 'The Lady is ready to watch *Family Feud.*' And then we'll watch our show together and have supper together, and that's all you need to do for me. If I get Alzheimer's or dementia, you can move another woman into the apartment like B. Smith's husband did. I won't know who she is and I want you to be happy."

He asked, "Just so I know, what odds of survival are you *not* going to fight?"

I said, "Thirty percent, I'm out."

"Really? Not twenty?"

"Fine, if I have less than a twenty percent survival rate, I get to give up. Call hospice."

When I was in college, Grandpapa, Mama's father, moved into their house to die under the care of hospice, and from what I understand, the experience was positive. He had palliative care and was never in pain. The drugs let him sleep. He could smell an azalea bush outside the window. He had visitors. And then one morning, he was gone.

Years later, during one of my visits home, Papa asked me, "Helen Michelle, do you ever get the sense that your grandfather died in this room, in the bed where you sleep?"

"I do *now,*" I said.

"Don't worry. We changed the mattress."

My husband told me that he'd bet a thousand dollars that they did not.

On the other end of the death-defying spectrum, my friend Dani wants to live as long as possible no matter what the cost or what condition she's in.

"Understood," I said. "Twice a week, I'll visit your cryogenically frozen head in a jar."

"Perfect," she said. "And then after I'm dead, text my husband pictures of me every day forever and ever."

Dani's husband, Kevin, had to be formally voted into her family's "cemetery club" because there's only so much space. He won them over by saying he wants to make *Guinness World Records* for the world's shortest funeral.

He said, "Just have one guy stand up and say, 'He was a dick!' And then another guy stand up and say, 'He wasn't a dick!' That'll cover both sides. Funeral over."

I heard a funeral director say that the most common thing people are buried with is a pack of cigarettes slipped into a shirt pocket so that they won't have to go cold turkey in heaven. Granddaddy, Papa's father, was buried in his horn-rims so he could see. My parents had planned to donate their bodies to science, but the University of Alabama Medical Center has an age cutoff and their cadavers are no longer wanted. My sister and I joke that unless they figure out an alternative, we're going to have them stuffed like suits of armor. Turns out, the joke's on us. Recently, Mama told us she wants to be mulched.

She handed me a pamphlet with a picture of an older couple sitting in a forest. There is a business that will turn your body into fertilizer and dump you in the great outdoors.

Mama said, "I don't want any fuss when I die, Helen Michelle. Just have them pull up in a log truck and throw me in the back."

"Okay, Mama."

"If we buy in early, I get fifteen free saplings!"

"That is a good deal."

A friend told me, "All I need to know about what my parents want done when they die is in the *Box*."

The *Box* is in my friend's mother's bedroom closet. Inside the *Box* are receipts. Her parents have already paid a funeral home and picked out their caskets, bought cemetery plots and tombstones, chosen what flowers they want shaped into a horseshoe, what they want to wear, and what obituary photos to run.

Mama teases me that if she gets to choose my obituary photo, she'll choose the picture that she and Papa stapled to my kindergarten application for the one year I was in private school. The picture is of me in a petting zoo feeding a goat. On the back of the photo, Papa wrote, "Helen Michelle is the one on the left."

I told my husband, "I don't want a funeral, just burn me up."

My husband said, "That sounds scary to me."

"For you to watch?"

"No, I'm not going to watch. I mean scary for *you*. To be burned."

"I'm not scared, I won't know what's happening." I asked him, "What do *you* want me to do with you? Do you want to go in the mausoleum with the rest of your family?"

My husband's mother went in when he was seventeen. My husband's brother went in when he was twenty-five. My husband's father is not with them because after my husband's mother divorced him, he moved back to Greece and died there when my husband was a boy.

My husband said, "I guess cremation is okay. But I don't want you to keep my ashes."

"I don't want you to keep my ashes either."

"But I want casseroles from people."

"So, you'll have a reception."

If my husband can't bring himself to respect my end-of-life wishes, I know he'll take good care of me because for years I watched him take good care of his grandmother. Every day, he walked a block from our apartment to her apartment and visited with her before he went to work, and then visited with her after work. He did the same when she was in and out of hospitals. She spent one night in a nursing home, and that one night was all that she and my husband could stand. He hired round-the-clock sitters—and *sitters* is what they were with no medical training, but the ability to dial 911, which they did one night while my husband and I were watching Donald Sutherland in a play at Lincoln Center, and by the time EMTs and we got to Yiayia, she was gone.

My husband entrusted her body to the same funeral home that took care of Jacqueline Kennedy Onassis. Yia-yia's hair was styled and her makeup artfully applied. Her dress was not expensive, but she was dressed like a first lady. She didn't ask for this. But my husband showed her that life, even after death, can be full of surprises.

Obituary of a First Kiss

high school friend texted me the obituary of my first kiss. She didn't remember that he was my first kiss and it took me a beat to remember that he was the best friend of her first kiss. Then we remembered that he'd also been a boyfriend of another friend of ours. He was a funny redheaded sophomore who was one year older than us, and he had a car. Our friend's father had disapproved of him—because he was one year older than us and had a car—so our friend snuck out of her bedroom window to meet him and snuck him in through her bedroom window to kiss.

I think this boy took me to a dance after they dated, but that couldn't be right. I can't believe I'd go on a date with my friend's boyfriend, even after they broke up. But then, I can't believe he'd have asked me out on a date before her. My guess is that it had been an arrangement. Some kind of friendship thing, but he and I were never friends. We were *friendly.* We had friends in common. I didn't have a crush on him.

I think there is a photo of us dressed for some sort of Sadie Hawkins or spring fling kind of thing. I know it wasn't prom. We were too young to go to prom. In my memory *of a memory* of a photo, I wore a silk plaid dress with puffy short sleeves, black sheer pantyhose with a reinforced toe, and black flats. He wore suspenders, white parachute pants, and a hot pink tie. But I might be remembering his face on the body of the boy who I *wished* was my first kiss, but who would be my second kiss.

Maybe I'd been on a date with this boy who would be my second kiss, but this boy, who was my first kiss, was the boy who'd driven everyone on our double date home. Maybe I was last to be dropped off. Whatever the case, he parked his car by my mailbox and walked me up the short path to my front door.

I don't know if he kissed me out of pity, curiosity, desire, or because he was a kisser. Some boys just like to kiss. And he was a great kisser. He hugged me, drew back, and then we were kissing. Under the safety of my porch light, we were spotlighted for all the neighbors to see if they looked out their windows at a time that wasn't later than my ten o'clock curfew.

The kiss was everything I'd hoped for: soft, then searching. Caught up in his arms, my back pressed against the bricks of my house, my shoe soles slipped on the painted cement. The kiss happened so easily. I never felt scared. I only felt bold. I can still feel my body lit up with electricity when I think of that kiss thirty-eight years later.

I crept up the carpeted stairs to my room and lay in my bed on top of the covers. I went to sleep in my dress because I could smell his Drakkar Noir in the silk. I replayed the kiss until I drifted off to sleep. I woke up thinking about it.

My high school friend who texted me his obituary hadn't remembered he was my first kiss. She texted, "I am sorry to spring it on you. My bad."

I texted, "Just a nice one-night memory. Kissing on a front porch. After a dance I think."

My relationship with this boy never went any further. We never went on another date. We never kissed a second time. He never knew he was my first kiss. Maybe I never told my friend about it when we were girls. Maybe I never told anyone.

But I told my husband, "My first kiss died."

He said, "You're not going to tell me he was the best kiss you ever had, are you?"

"No, no, no. Just the first. You know, you always remember your first kiss."

I showed him the picture of the boy that *The Tuscaloosa*

News had published. The boy was a fifty-three-year-old man with kind eyes and a purple tie.

I asked my husband, "Who was your first kiss?"

He said her name.

It took some coaxing to get the story out of him. My husband is not one for lengthy descriptions. He's a newsman and speaks in headlines. Half of our conversations are me saying, "Go on."

My husband said, "It was at school. It was outside. She'd waited for me after a dance. I'd had no idea she was interested in me and then we were walking and she swung around and kissed me."

"*She* kissed *you*?"

"She kissed me."

I asked, "What do you remember about it?"

He said, "I remember liking it."

I asked, "Do you remember *our* first kiss?"

"I do. It was on the street. It was at night. We were walking, and you swung around and kissed me."

"*I* kissed *you*?"

"You kissed me."

"I thought *you* kissed *me*!"

"You kissed me."

I said, "I remember I *asked* you if you wanted to kiss me at the restaurant beforehand."

"I remember that."

I said, "I was so young and full of myself. I thought I was

so seductive. I remember saying to you, 'Is this the part of the evening when you lean across the table and kiss me?' "

"Yep."

"And you said, 'No.' "

"I remember it sounding like a line you'd used before."

"It was," I said. "And you're the only guy who ever said no."

"Yeah, I was pretty proud of myself."

"So I thought for sure *you'd* kissed *me.* You know, after giving me that line about how you were going to spoil me so I'd never want to date another tall man again."

"Yeah, that was a line. But *you* kissed *me.*"

I asked, "What do you remember about the kiss?"

He said, "I remember liking it."

Me, I remember that kiss having a tranquilizing effect. Like a dart. *Smack.* My arms went limp and I was into him. I was wearing a black dress with white flowers. Or was it a black pleated skirt and stretchy collared cardigan that I'd buttoned all the way up to the neck? I'm sure I was wearing the same brand of Hanes Silk Reflections I'd been wearing since ninth grade. Maybe a two-inch chunky heel. Or were they Dr. Martens because it *was* the 1990s?

The kiss was in the Village, near my favorite mystery bookstore—Partners & Crime—that would later close because of a flood (or maybe it just folded). Or did he kiss me on Houston Street between Arturo's Pizza and the Film Forum (places we still go all the time)? Did I smell powdered sugar coming off fried zeppole from the Feast of San Gennaro? No, that couldn't be right, that festival is in mid-September and we kissed late in August.

I know our kiss was lit by streetlights. Our feet were on concrete. There were people everywhere—brushing past us and talking; laughing and shouting in the distance. There were cars and car alarms, dogs barking, music and *competing* music. Noise. New York City is noisy. But everything went quiet when he kissed me.

He says *I* kissed *him,* but my husband can still kiss me the way I remember him kissing me for the first time that night. Somehow sedate me and elate me. Make me open to his ideas. I'm not talking about a peck. I mean a *real* kiss. One that feels like he's put some thought into it. Or better yet, no thought at all.

I remember our first kiss better than I remember our wedding kiss. In all honesty, I don't remember our wedding kiss (who can kiss worth a damn in front of a Greek priest and your parents?). I don't remember New Year's Eve kisses either. Or any others that are meant to mark special occasions.

But I remember my husband's kisses in Paris, where we went for our ten-year anniversary because, instead of the French double kiss (one kiss on each cheek), he gave me four kisses (one kiss on each cheek, *twice*). In winter, he gives me what I call "warm lips, cold nose" because his nose is so "prominent" it presses into my cheek. When he kisses me with Nicorette, he tongues the gum between his cheek and teeth. When we get into bed, he puts on his sleep mask, folds his hands over his chest, puckers, and blindly waits for me to kiss him goodnight. I kiss him. And then he puckers again. Sometimes, many times.

Pucker. Pucker. Pucker.

Smooch. Smooch. Smooch.

My husband says he remembers kissing me in a dark booth at what's now Match 65 Brasserie. He remembers kissing me over a Scrabble board. He remembers kissing me on East Eighty-Fifth Street when I got off an Atlantic City bus with a big casino payout check in hand. He remembers kissing me to CDs: k. d. lang's *Ingénue,* Steely Dan's *Can't Buy a Thrill,* and the soundtrack to *Stealing Beauty.*

My husband has kissed me tens of thousands of times in our apartment. In our bedroom, our kitchen, our living room, and the Coral Lounge. And these kisses add up. We have accumulated kisses. When times get tough, we have kisses to fall back on.

For twenty-eight years, we have kissed only each other.

I asked him, "Can you believe our first kiss is our *last* first kiss? That is until one of us dies or commits adultery."

My husband assured me, "It's our last first kiss."

Oh, I kissed him for that line.

Or did *he* kiss *me*?

This is how memory works in a happy marriage. We remember what's romantic, what's funny, what's honest, what's sweet. We are writing our own love story. The best part is the heart.

Contract for a

Happy Marriage

*T*his agreement made November 9, 2001, is a living document, the terms of which may be changed at any time at the sole discretion of the party of the first part (hereafter known as "Mr.") and the party of the second part (hereafter known as "Mrs.").

Mr. will go to the theater with Mrs. on the condition that the runtime is ninety minutes without intermission, has full-frontal nudity, or stars Laurie Metcalf. No more brunches or "going to see a baby." No vow renewals, surprise parties, or "over the top" attempts at seduction since the 2002 candlelit rose petal path that Mr. found "so spooky" he backed out of the apartment and asked a doorman to investigate. Thanksgiving is for listening to "Alice's Restaurant" on WFUV and putting up the Christmas tree. Christmas is for going to the movies. New Year's Eve is for going to bed early. No "doing" anything for the summer.

No churchgoing, but don't put anything in front of Yiayia's religious icon on the second shelf in Mr.'s closet.

Due to an influx of stickers, the glitter drawer has been downsized to share a craft box with inkpads and rubber stamps. If a cleaning tool has not been used in a year since purchase, it will be disposed of like the "Wet Pet Suck Vac" of 2020 and the Four Piece Hardwood Floor Care System of 2018. If a gathering for more than fifty guests is not thrown for a third consecutive year, ten boxes of wineglasses will be removed from the storage bin and donated to charity. Same goes for the red Igloo coolers, but the Bed Bath & Beyond plastic bucket with a price sticker that says "tub ass" will be kept for sentimental reasons.

Don't Let Me See How You Get Rid of It, Just Get Rid of It Amendment: If Mr. must throw away an item that belongs to Mrs., he must do so out of her line of sight. See: The 2017 flood-stained rugs needlepointed by Grandpapa; the 2021 cat-piss-soaked curtain that was more expensive to dry-clean than to replace; three framed posters purchased in Athens in 2002 that are of Greek translations of "classic" American movies now seen as "problematic"; and a 997-piece jigsaw puzzle. Addendum: Don't let Mrs. see the industrial black trash bag used to haul off her stuff.

Casseroles are limited in production because of 2016 high cholesterol scores. Salads are in, but that yellow salad dressing is out. Fondue is out. Crumbled goat cheese on everything is out. Potato chips for dessert are encouraged.

Since the 2015 kitchen renovation, the cabinets to the left and right of the oven are stained from heat, the walls stained with cat food juice because both parties opted for matte paint instead of glossy, and there is a crack in a floor tile—which both parties have agreed not to discuss—so the Anti-Splatter Amendment of 2015 has been repealed and orange chicken is back on the menu. Addendum: Mr. acknowledges Mrs. is not a nutritionist and can't be expected to know that egg-battered floured fried chicken bits are just as bad as casseroles. All nightly meals for both parties will continue to be prepared by or ordered by Mrs., but if she is sick, Mr. will cook her a hamburger patty. Due to the success of Three Cake Week in 2022, Mr. will bake a box cake when Mrs. is "feeling forlorn."

Because I'm Worth It Amendment: If a pandemic lockdown reaches a two-month mark, Mr. will dye Mrs.'s grey roots. Mrs. agrees not to sob uncontrollably as if she is being deloused, nor afterward complain that the hair on the top of her head is so much darker than what's below her ears, she looks like she's wearing a ski cap. She further agrees to not point out brunette splotches on the shower curtain and wallpaper. She will verbalize a "thank-you" and acknowledge that Mr. "did his best."

After finishing the daily *New York Times* crossword on the toilet, Mrs. will not drop her Bic on the bathroom floor like a mic and leave it for Mr. to step on barefooted when he pees while she "sleeps like an angel" in the middle of the night. Mr. agrees to clip his nails with the bathroom door shut but is allowed to floss his teeth "free range" while watching "his Danish shows" on Netflix in the Coral Lounge.

While watching TV as a couple, Mr. agrees to fast-forward, mute, and narrate the "gross stuff" for Mrs. in exchange for Mrs. rubbing his feet in the presence of housewives, house hunters, haunted house–hunters, hoarders, or 1970s sitcom stars turned celebrity chefs. No subtitles for southern accents. No scenes from next week. Crying is to be expected from Mr. and accepted by Mrs. when Mr. rewatches *Saturday Night Fever* or any episode from the first two seasons of *Friday Night Lights.*

Made for TV Clause: If this book is adapted for the small screen, Mr. gets to cast the actor who plays him. Contenders include Chris Meloni, Stanley Tucci, Don Cheadle, and Brian Tyree Henry.

For the Material Clause: Mrs. will not "pressure" Mr. to do things so that she can have something to write about. Those activities may include, but are not limited to, bungee jumping, ziplining, flea markets, corn mazes, sadomasochistic role-play, "anything on a boat," or "leaving the city to do something he can do *in* the city." Addendum: Mr. agrees that Mrs. may take one photo of him a year "doing something he doesn't normally do for her amusement." See: 2006 photo of Mr. in a naked torso apron; 2015 photo

CONTRACT FOR A HAPPY MARRIAGE

of Mr. perched atop a sculpture of a gigantic snail; and 2011 photo of Mr. "smelling the roses." Addendum: As of April 8, 2022, Mr. is released from his photo obligation for a period of two years because—as a gift for Mrs. (entirely unprompted by her and outside of her presence)—Mr. took a photo of himself on the Hollywood Walk of Fame beside Joan Collins's star.

Neighbors may be spied on through the peephole. If they are drunk and leave their keys in the common hallway, Mrs. agrees not to steal said keys in order to "teach them a lesson." If neighbors are threatening divorce and the wife throwing her husband's clothes, shoes, and L.L. Bean monogrammed tote bag into the common hallway, Mrs. agrees not to call the police, super, or report such building violations to the co-op board, but Mr. agrees to let Mrs. take a picture of said stuff to use as ammunition when said neighbors email them to complain about Mr.'s kick scooter left in the hallway.

Let It Sit Like a Hot Roast Clause: Both parties agree to stop the other from replying to emails in a manner that will "make them look like the crazy one."

Rip It Off Like a Band-Aid Clause: Both parties agree that when one of them comes home from a doctor's appointment with a Band-Aid, the other gets to rip it off.

Alien Invasion Clause: If UFOs attack, both parties agree to walk out of their apartment building and be "taken."

Nuclear Bomb Clause: If Manhattan is hit by "the big one," both parties agree not to bother shutting the windows to survive it.

Serial Killer Clause: If a box of "souvenirs" is found, said souvenirs will be turned over to the police.

Catchphrase Clause: Both parties may say what the other one says. For example, Mr. may say, "Can you *imagine*?" "Tell me *everything*," and "Enjoyable!" and Mrs. may say, "That sounds like a personal problem" and "Fair enough."

Mr. agrees to quit telling Mrs. what time it is on an hourly basis. Mr. agrees to quit telling Mrs. how much he weighs on a daily basis. Mr. agrees to quit asking Mrs. what smells so bad—if and when he smells something bad—because the answer is always the same: the cat pooped in the tub.

Mrs. will "try" not to scream like she's riding the Scrambler at a state fair when—to her surprise—Mr. enters a room. Mrs. agrees to quit saying, "WHAT?" in the tone of a woman expecting news of the apocalypse when Mr. asks her, "Guess what?"

Mrs. agrees to quit asking, "DID YOU?" As in:

Mrs.: "Did you lock the front door?"

Mr.: "Yes."

Mrs.: "DID YOU?"

Talking to dogs on the street is out, talking to cats in the apartment is tolerated. Talking to babies on the street is out, talking to babies on Zoom is "okay for now." Talking to airplane seatmates is out unless Mr. is in the middle seat and being "engaged with" by a stranger and needs Mrs. to "put a stop to it." No sampling flavors at ice cream parlors, "just roll the dice."

Both parties agree and are comfortable with the fact that it's too late for them to learn a second language or understand what "alternate side parking" is.

Both parties agree to buy generic OTC drugs, trash bags, sour cream, and bricks of cheddar but pay full price for Bounty, Charmin, Tide, Dawn, Windex, Clorox, Kleenex, Scrubbing Bubbles, and Ruffles.

Mr. will do all laundry and clean the cat box. Mrs. will "handle" cat barf, cat pee *outside the box,* health insurance, social outings, and home intruders that include but are not limited to ants, roaches, spiders, flies, "house centipedes," mice, and men. No "obvious" weapons in the apartment.

When Mr. comes home, he must announce himself with a "Hello!"

When Mr. comes into view of Mrs., she promises to never stop saying, "Handsome!"

Failure by either party to comply with any of these terms will be known as a "breach of contract." There are no penalties, but both parties promise each other to never stop trying.

Mr. _____

Mrs. _____

ACKNOWLEDGMENTS

This book would not exist if Lex Haris did not marry me. Or if Brettne Bloom did not tell me to write a book about my marriage. Or if Jenny Jackson did not curate the best parts of my heart. Ann Napolitano and Hannah Tinti watched me fall in love with Lex, arranged the seat cards at our wedding supper, and have stood by me—joining our writing lives together—for better or for worse. My parents and my sister and her family are an endless inspiration. My friends are my muses. The New York Society Library is my sanctuary. Doubleday is the house where I can be myself.

Enjoyable!

ABOUT THE AUTHOR

HELEN ELLIS is the author of *Bring Your Baggage and Don't Pack Light, Southern Lady Code, American Housewife,* and *Eating the Cheshire Cat.* Raised in Alabama, she lives with her husband in New York City. She is a poker player and a plant lady. You can find her on Twitter @WhatIDoAllDay and Instagram @HelenEllisAuthor.